Low-FODMAP Diet

Cookbook for Beginners UK

Nutritious and Simple Low-FODMAP Recipes to Soothe Your Gut and Enhance Digestive Wellness, Unlock the Secrets to a Balanced Gut

Reece Rice

CONTENTS

Meat Recipes 27

Vegetarian And Vegan Recipes 40

Soups, Salads And Sides Recipes 52

Sauces, Dressings, And Condiments Recipes 63

Snacks & Desserts Recipes 72

INTRODUCTION

Hello everyone, I am thrilled to introduce my latest cookbook, "Low-FODMAP Diet Cookbook for Beginners UK." My name is Reece Rice, and I am a passionate food enthusiast and a certified nutritionist. Over the years, I have witnessed the profound impact that diet has on our overall well-being, particularly on gut health. This realization inspired me to create this cookbook, filled with nutritious and simple low-FODMAP recipes.

As someone who has personally struggled with digestive issues, I understand the frustration and discomfort that comes with them. I have spent years researching and experimenting with various diets, trying to find a solution that would alleviate my symptoms. It was during this journey that I discovered the Low-FODMAP diet. By following a low-FODMAP diet, individuals can identify and eliminate trigger foods, leading to improved gut health and reduced symptoms.

"Low-FODMAP Diet Cookbook for Beginners UK" is specifically tailored for beginners, making it accessible to anyone who is new to the low-FODMAP diet. The recipes are simple, straightforward, and do not require extensive culinary skills or hard-to-find ingredients. Each recipe is accompanied by detailed instructions and nutritional information, ensuring that you can easily prepare delicious and gut-friendly meals.

Furthermore, this cookbook offers a diverse range of recipes that cater to different tastes and dietary preferences. From breakfast options, such as hearty smoothies and comforting porridges, to satisfying main courses and delightful desserts, there is something for everyone. The recipes feature a variety of ingredients, including lean proteins, whole grains, fresh fruits and vegetables, and gut-friendly herbs and spices. This ensures that you can enjoy a balanced and nutritious diet while soothing their gut.

By following the recipes and guidance in "Low-FODMAP Diet Cookbook for Beginners UK," you can expect to experience a significant improvement in their gut health and overall well-being. You will learn to prepare delicious meals that are gentle on their digestive system, reducing symptoms such as bloating, gas, and abdominal pain. Additionally, you will gain a better understanding of your own body's response to different foods, allowing you to make informed choices and personalize their diet for optimal gut health.

Let's embark on this gut-healing journey together and discover the joy of nourishing and delicious low-FODMAP meals!

What is the Low-FODMAP Diet exactly?

The Low-FODMAP Diet is a dietary approach that aims to reduce the intake of certain carbohydrates called FOD-MAPs (fermentable oligosaccharides, disaccharides, monosaccharides, and polyols) to alleviate symptoms in people with irritable bowel syndrome (IBS) or other digestive disorders.

FODMAPs are a group of poorly absorbed carbohydrates that can cause digestive symptoms such as bloating, gas, abdominal pain, diarrhea, or constipation in some individuals, particularly those with sensitive digestive systems. FODMAPs include fermentable sugars like lactose, fructose, and sorbitol, as well as certain types of fiber.

The Low-FODMAP Diet involves a strict elimination phase, during which high-FODMAP foods are avoided for a specific period, usually 2-6 weeks. This phase aims to reduce symptoms by minimizing the intake of FODMAPs. After the elimination phase, a reintroduction phase follows, where FODMAP-containing foods are gradually reintroduced to identify specific triggers and determine individual tolerance levels.

The Low-FODMAP Diet is not a long-term or permanent diet. Its purpose is to identify and manage trigger foods that may worsen digestive symptoms. Once trigger foods are identified, a person can create a personalized diet that avoids high-FODMAP foods while including a wide variety of other nutritious options.

What are some benefits of a Low-FODMAP Diet?

The Low-FODMAP Diet can provide several benefits for individuals with irritable bowel syndrome (IBS) or other digestive disorders. Here are some potential benefits of following a Low-FODMAP Diet:

• **Reduces digestive symptoms**

The primary goal of the Low-FODMAP Diet is to alleviate digestive symptoms such as bloating, gas, abdominal pain, diarrhea, or constipation, which are common in individuals with IBS. By avoiding high-FODMAP foods, which can trigger symptoms in sensitive individuals, the diet can help reduce or even eliminate these symptoms, improving overall quality of life.

• **Identifies trigger foods**

Following the Low-FODMAP Diet involves an elimination phase, during which high-FODMAP foods are avoided for a specific period. After this phase, individual foods are gradually reintroduced to identify trigger foods that may worsen symptoms. This helps individuals understand their personal tolerance levels and develop a customized diet plan that avoids specific FODMAPs that trigger their symptoms.

• **Provides a sense of control**

IBS and other digestive disorders can significantly impact daily life and cause discomfort and anxiety. The Low-FODMAP Diet gives individuals a sense of control over their symptoms by providing a structured approach to identify and manage trigger foods. This can lead to increased confidence and a better understanding of how to manage their condition.

• **Improves gut health**

While the Low-FODMAP Diet restricts certain carbohydrates, it encourages the consumption of other gut-friendly foods, such as low-FODMAP fruits, vegetables, whole grains, lean proteins, and healthy fats. These foods provide essential nutrients, fiber, and beneficial compounds that support overall gut health, including gut microbiota diversity.

• **Supports nutrient intake**

The Low-FODMAP Diet can be nutritionally balanced if followed correctly. While certain high-FODMAP foods are restricted, there are still plenty of nutrient-dense options available. Working with a registered dietitian can ensure that nutrient needs are met through appropriate food choices and, if needed, the use of suitable supplements.

• **Enhances overall well-being**

By reducing or eliminating digestive symptoms, the Low-FODMAP Diet can improve overall well-being and quality of life. It can lead to better sleep, increased energy levels, reduced anxiety related to food choices, and improved social interactions, as individuals can participate more comfortably in activities involving food.

What to Eat on The Low-FODMAP Diet?

On the low-FODMAP diet, it is recommended to avoid or limit certain types of carbohydrates that can be difficult to digest. Here are some foods that are generally safe to eat on a low-FODMAP diet:

Proteins: Chicken, turkey, fish, tofu, tempeh, eggs, and lactose-free dairy products like lactose-free milk, yogurt, and cheese.

Grains: Gluten-free grains like rice, quinoa, oats, and corn. Avoid wheat, barley, and rye.

Fruits: Bananas, blueberries, strawberries, oranges, grapes, and pineapple in small portions. Limit high-FODMAP fruits like apples, pears, and cherries.

Vegetables: Carrots, spinach, bell peppers, zucchini, cucumber, lettuce, and tomatoes. Limit onion, garlic, cauliflower, and broccoli.

Nuts and seeds: Almonds (in moderation), walnuts, sunflower seeds, and pumpkin seeds.

Condiments and sweeteners: Olive oil, coconut oil, balsamic vinegar, maple syrup (in moderation), and small amounts of low-FODMAP herbs and spices.

Beverages: Water, herbal tea, coffee (in moderation), and lactose-free milk.

Can I still enjoy a varied and balanced diet while following the Low-FODMAP Diet?

Yes, it is possible to enjoy a varied and balanced diet while following the low-FODMAP diet. Although some high-FODMAP foods need to be limited or avoided, there are still plenty of options available to create nutritious and diverse meals. Here are some tips to ensure a varied and balanced diet while following the low-FOD-MAP diet:

• Include a variety of low-FODMAP fruits and vegetables

While some high-FODMAP fruits and vegetables need to be limited, there are still many low-FODMAP options to enjoy. Incorporate a variety of colorful fruits and vegetables into your diet to ensure you are getting a range of nutrients.

• Choose gluten-free grains

Wheat, barley, and rye contain FODMAPs and should be avoided. However, there are many gluten-free grains that are low in FODMAPs, such as rice, quinoa, oats, and corn. These grains can be used as a base for meals and provide a good source of carbohydrates.

• Include lean proteins

Protein is an essential part of a balanced diet. Opt for lean sources of protein like chicken, turkey, fish, tofu, and eggs. These can be prepared in various ways to add variety to your meals.

• Incorporate lactose-free dairy

If you tolerate lactose, include lactose-free dairy products like lactose-free milk, yogurt, and cheese in your diet. These provide a good source of calcium and other important nutrients.

• Explore alternative sources of calcium

If you cannot tolerate lactose or choose to avoid dairy, there are other sources of calcium available. Some low-FODMAP options include lactose-free fortified plant-based milk, calcium-fortified tofu, and canned fish with bones like salmon or sardines.

• Experiment with herbs and spices

While some spices and herbs can be high in FODMAPs, many are low-FODMAP and can add flavor to your meals. Experiment with low-FODMAP herbs and spices like basil, oregano, thyme, turmeric, and ginger to enhance the taste of your dishes.

• Include healthy fats

Fats are an important part of a balanced diet. Include healthy fats like olive oil, coconut oil, avocado, and nuts (in moderation) to provide essential fatty acids.

• Stay hydrated

Water is essential for overall health. Make sure to drink enough water throughout the day. You can also enjoy low-FODMAP beverages like herbal tea, coffee (in moderation), and lactose-free milk.

• Plan your meals ahead

Planning your meals ahead of time can help ensure you have a variety of low-FODMAP options available. This will prevent you from getting stuck in a monotonous routine.

Measurement Conversions

BASIC KITCHEN CONVERSIONS & EQUIVALENTS

DRY MEASUREMENTS CONVERSION CHART

3 TEASPOONS = 1 TABLESPOON = 1/16 CUP

6 TEASPOONS = 2 TABLESPOONS = 1/8 CUP

12 TEASPOONS = 4 TABLESPOONS = 1/4 CUP

24 TEASPOONS = 8 TABLESPOONS = 1/2 CUP

36 TEASPOONS = 12 TABLESPOONS = 3/4 CUP

48 TEASPOONS = 16 TABLESPOONS = 1 CUP

METRIC TO US COOKING CONVERSIONS

OVEN TEMPERATURES

120 °C = 250 °F

160 °C = 320 °F

180° C = 350 °F

205 °C = 400 °F

220 °C = 425 °F

LIQUID MEASUREMENTS CONVERSION CHART

8 FLUID OUNCES = 1 CUP = 1/2 PINT = 1/4 QUART

16 FLUID OUNCES = 2 CUPS = 1 PINT = 1/2 QUART

32 FLUID OUNCES = 4 CUPS = 2 PINTS = 1 QUART

 = 1/4 GALLON

128 FLUID OUNCES = 16 CUPS = 8 PINTS = 4 QUARTS = 1 GALLON

BAKING IN GRAMS

1 CUP FLOUR = 140 GRAMS

1 CUP SUGAR = 150 GRAMS

1 CUP POWDERED SUGAR = 160 GRAMS

1 CUP HEAVY CREAM = 235 GRAMS

VOLUME

1 MILLILITER = 1/5 TEASPOON

5 ML = 1 TEASPOON

15 ML = 1 TABLESPOON

240 ML = 1 CUP OR 8 FLUID OUNCES

1 LITER = 34 FL. OUNCES

WEIGHT

1 GRAM = .035 OUNCES

100 GRAMS = 3.5 OUNCES

500 GRAMS = 1.1 POUNDS

1 KILOGRAM = 35 OUNCES

US TO METRIC COOKING CONVERSIONS

1/5 TSP = 1 ML

1 TSP = 5 ML

1 TBSP = 15 ML

1 FL OUNCE = 30 ML

1 CUP = 237 ML

1 PINT (2 CUPS) = 473 ML

1 QUART (4 CUPS) = .95 LITER

1 GALLON (16 CUPS) = 3.8 LITERS

1 OZ = 28 GRAMS

1 POUND = 454 GRAMS

BUTTER

1 CUP BUTTER = 2 STICKS = 8 OUNCES = 230 GRAMS = 8 TABLESPOONS

WHAT DOES 1 CUP EQUAL

1 CUP = 8 FLUID OUNCES

1 CUP = 16 TABLESPOONS

1 CUP = 48 TEASPOONS

1 CUP = 1/2 PINT

1 CUP = 1/4 QUART

1 CUP = 1/16 GALLON

1 CUP = 240 ML

BAKING PAN CONVERSIONS

1 CUP ALL-PURPOSE FLOUR = 4.5 OZ

1 CUP ROLLED OATS = 3 OZ 1 LARGE EGG = 1.7 OZ

1 CUP BUTTER = 8 OZ 1 CUP MILK = 8 OZ

1 CUP HEAVY CREAM = 8.4 OZ

1 CUP GRANULATED SUGAR = 7.1 OZ

1 CUP PACKED BROWN SUGAR = 7.75 OZ

1 CUP VEGETABLE OIL = 7.7 OZ

1 CUP UNSIFTED POWDERED SUGAR = 4.4 OZ

BAKING PAN CONVERSIONS

9-INCH ROUND CAKE PAN = 12 CUPS

10-INCH TUBE PAN =16 CUPS

11-INCH BUNDT PAN = 12 CUPS

9-INCH SPRINGFORM PAN = 10 CUPS

9 X 5 INCH LOAF PAN = 8 CUPS

9-INCH SQUARE PAN = 8 CUPS

Breakfast & Brunch Recipes

Mixed Berry & Yogurt Granola Bar

Servings:12
Cooking Time: 30 Minutes
Ingredients:

- 2 cups rolled oats
- 3 tbsp shredded coconut
- 2 tbsp macadamia nut meal
- 4 tbsp chia seeds
- 1 egg (whites only)
- ⅓ cup peanut oil
- ¼ cup maple syrup
- 1 cup mixed berries
- 1 ½ cups Greek yogurt
- 3 tbsp white chocolate, melted

Directions:

1. Preheat the oven to 375°F. Line a baking tray with parchment paper.
2. Mix the ingredients in a bowl, and then press into the pan. Bake for 30 minutes.
3. Allow to cool, then drizzle with chocolate and serve.

Nutrition:

- Info784g Calories, 9.5g Total fat, 3.2g Saturated fat, 18.5g Carbohydrates, 2.8 g Fiber, 3.9g Protein, 6.4g Sodium.

Potato Pancakes

Servings:4
Cooking Time: 10 Minutes
Ingredients:

- 3 medium potatoes, peeled and quartered
- 2 eggs
- 2 tablespoons rice flour
- ½ teaspoon salt
- ¼ teaspoon freshly ground pepper
- 2 tablespoons coconut or grapeseed oil

Directions:

1. In a blender or food processor, pulse the potatoes until they are finely chopped.
2. In a medium bowl, whisk the eggs, and then add the flour, salt, pepper, and the finely chopped potatoes, and stir to mix well.
3. Heat the oil in a large skillet over medium-high heat. Add the potato mixture about ¼ cup at a time, using the back of a spoon or scoop to flatten into pancakes about 3 inches in diameter. Cook for 3 to 4 minutes per side, until the pancakes are golden brown and crisp. Serve hot.

Nutrition:

- InfoCalories: 169; Protein: 6g; Total Fat: 3g; Saturated Fat: 2g; Carbohydrates: 30g; Fiber: 4g; Sodium: 332mg;

Ginger-berry Rice Milk Smoothie

Servings:2
Cooking Time: None
Ingredients:

- 2 cups frozen strawberries, blueberries, or raspberries
- 1 cup unsweetened rice milk
- 2 tablespoons maple syrup
- 2 teaspoons finely grated fresh ginger
- 2 teaspoons lemon juice

Directions:

1. Place all of the ingredients in a blender and blend until smooth.
2. Serve immediately.

Nutrition Info:

- InfoCalories: 162; Protein: 2g; Total Fat: 2g; Saturated Fat: 0g; Carbohydrates: 37g; Fiber: 8g;

Blueberry Lime Smoothie

Servings:1
Cooking Time: 3 Minutes
Ingredients:
- ½ cup blueberries, fresh or frozen
- 2 tbsp coconut flakes
- 2 tbsp lime juice, fresh
- ½ cup Greek or lactose-free yogurt
- 1 tsp chia seeds
- 2 tbsp water
- Ice (only if using fresh blueberries and if you want a thicker consistency)

Directions:
1. Place ingredients in a blender and mix until it starts to look frothy.

Nutrition Info:
- Info319g Calories, 23g Total fat, 7g Saturated fat, 26g Carbohydrates, 6 g Fiber, 7g Protein, 15g Sodium.

Tomato Omelet

Servings:2
Cooking Time: 5 Minutes
Ingredients:
- 4 fresh tomatoes
- 4 eggs
- ¼ cup water
- ½ tsp chopped basil
- Pinch of salt
- Pinch of pepper
- 2 tbsp olive oil (or other approved oil)

Directions:
1. Place a pot of water on the stove and bring to a boil. Mark each tomato with an 'x' in the skin and place them in the water. Leave the tomatoes in the water for 30 seconds before removing them with a draining spoon and placing them into cold water.
2. Peel the skin off the tomatoes and cut them in half. Remove the core and seeds and slice into strips. Set them aside.
3. Break the eggs into a bowl and whisk together while adding the basil, salt, and pepper. Stop whisking when the mixture is frothy. Place the mixture into a hot pan that has been greased with oil.
4. Gently stir the mixture while cooking over medium heat. When the mixture starts to get firm, spread the tomato over it. Do not continue stirring the mixture. When the tomatoes are warmed through, remove from the pan and enjoy.

Nutrition Info:
- Info311.5g Calories, 24g Total fat, 5g Saturated fat, 10.5g Carbohydrates, 3 g Fiber, 15g Protein, 7g Sodium.

Green Smoothie

Servings:1
Cooking Time: 0 Minutes
Ingredients:
- ½ cup fresh pineapple, chopped and then frozen
- 2 tablespoons baby spinach
- ¼ cup Greek yogurt
- 1 tbsp shredded coconut
- 2 tsp chia seeds
- ¼ cup almond milk
- 6 ice cubes

Directions:
1. Blend all the ingredients, except for the ice and milk.
2. Add the ice and blend.
3. Add the milk and continue blending until smooth.

Nutrition Info:
- Info347g Calories, 24g Total fat, 16g Saturated fat, 31g Carbohydrates, 10 g Fiber, 8g Protein, 17g Sodium.

Breakfast Ratatouille With Poached Eggs

Servings:4
Cooking Time: 40 Minutes
Ingredients:

- 2 tablespoons butter
- 1 medium eggplant, diced
- 4 medium tomatoes, peeled, seeded, and diced
- 1 red bell pepper, diced
- 1 green bell pepper, diced
- 2 medium zucchini, diced
- ½ cup halved artichoke hearts
- 1 jalapeño, diced
- 2 tablespoons chopped fresh thyme
- 1 tablespoon chopped fresh oregano
- ¼ cup chopped parsley
- ½ cup homemade (onion- and garlic-free) chicken or vegetable broth
- 1 teaspoon salt
- ½ teaspoon freshly ground pepper
- 4 eggs
- 2 ounces freshly grated Parmesan cheese

Directions:

1. Heat the butter in a large skillet over medium-high heat. Add the eggplant and cook, stirring occasionally, for about 10 minutes, until the eggplant is tender. Add the tomatoes and cook for about 5 minutes, until the tomatoes have begun to break down.
2. Add the bell peppers, zucchini, artichoke hearts, jalapeño, thyme, oregano, and parsley. Stir to mix. Add the broth, salt, and pepper, and bring to a boil. Cover, reduce the heat to low, and simmer for about 20 minutes, until the liquid has evaporated and the vegetables are tender.
3. While the vegetables are cooking, poach the eggs. Bring a pan of water about 3 inches deep to a boil over high heat. Reduce the heat to low, carefully break the eggs into the water, and simmer for 4 minutes.
4. To serve, ladle the vegetable mixture into 4 serving bowls, top each with a poached egg, and sprinkle the cheese over the top. Serve hot.

Nutrition Info:

- InfoCalories: 292; Protein: 21g; Total Fat: 15g; Saturated Fat: 7g; Carbohydrates: 24g; Fiber: 10g; Sodium: 819mg;

Tomato And Green Bean Salad

Servings:6
Cooking Time: 5 Minutes
Ingredients:

- 1 cup green beans
- ½ cup mayonnaise
- ½ cup Greek yogurt
- 1 tbsp chopped basil
- 2 tbsp chopped parsley
- Pinch of salt
- Pinch of pepper
- 2 tbsp lactose-free or another FODMAP-approved milk
- 1 tbsp Dijon mustard
- 2 tomatoes
- 2 spring onions, green part only
- 1 ½ cups lettuce

Directions:

1. In a bowl, mix mayonnaise, yogurt, milk, mustard, basil, parsley, salt, and pepper.
2. Wash the green beans, lettuce, and spring onions, then drain the water and chop the green onions. Shred the lettuce into a separate bowl and mix in the green beans and spring onions.
3. Cut the tomatoes into quarters and mix into the bowl. Put the dressing into a serving jug and serve.

Nutrition Info:

- Info125g Calories, 8.8g Total fat, 2g Saturated fat, 10.8g Carbohydrates, 1.8 g Fiber, 2.5g Protein, 4.5g Sodium.

Oysters, Three Ways

Servings:12
Cooking Time:x
Ingredients:

- 12 freshly shucked oysters, fully detached from and replaced on their shell
- CHEESE-CRUSTED
- 2 heaping tablespoons dried gluten-free, soy-free bread crumbs*
- 1 heaping tablespoon grated Parmesan
- 1 teaspoon finely chopped flat-leaf parsley
- 3½ ounces (100 g) Camembert, cut into 12 thin slices
- OYSTERS KILPATRICK
- 3 to 5 lean bacon slices (3½ ounces/100 g)
- ¼ cup (60 ml) gluten-free Worcestershire sauce*
- TOMATO AND CHILE
- 2 teaspoons garlic-infused olive oil
- ½ small red chile pepper, finely chopped
- ½ cup (125 ml) tomato puree

Directions:

1. Line a baking sheet with foil and place the oysters in their shells on the sheet. Preheat the broiler to high.
2. For cheese-crusted oysters, combine the bread crumbs, Parmesan, and parsley in a small bowl. Place a slice of Camembert on each oyster. Sprinkle the bread crumb mixture over the top.
3. For oysters Kilpatrick, cook the bacon until crisp. Drain on a paper towel and then chop finely. Place 1 teaspoon bacon and 1 teaspoon Worcestershire sauce on each oyster.
4. For tomato and chile oysters, heat the oil in a small frying pan over medium heat, add the chile pepper, and cook until softened. Stir in the tomato puree. Spoon the sauce evenly over the oysters.
5. Place the oysters under the broiler and cook for a few minutes until warmed through. Serve immediately, but be careful, because the shells will be hot!

Nutrition Info:

- Info: 19 calories,1 g protein,1 g total fat,2 g carbohydrates,66 mg sodiu.

Quiche In Ham Cups

Servings:6
Cooking Time: 20 Minutes
Ingredients:

- 6 slices ham, cold cut, rounded
- 1 small bell pepper, diced
- ½ cup spring onion, green tips only
- 4 eggs, beaten
- 2 tbsp rice flour
- 4 tbsp lactose-free milk, can be substituted with other approved milk
- Pinch of salt
- Pinch of pepper

Directions:

1. Preheat the oven to 350°F and line 6 muffin tins with the ham slices.
2. Mix together the flour and milk, whisking constantly.
3. Add in the eggs, salt, and pepper, mixing until smooth. Add the spring onion and bell pepper. Pour carefully into the ham cups.
4. Bake for 15-20 minutes. It's ready when the quiche is puffy and the ham is crispy.
5. Let cool for 10 minutes then use a knife to carefully lift the quiche out of the tins.

Nutrition Info:

- Info190g Calories, 8.5g Total fat, 5.1g Saturated fat, 11.8g Carbohydrates, 1.6 g Fiber, 9.5g Protein, 1.6g Sodium.

Fried Eggs With Potato Hash

Servings:2

Cooking Time: 26 Minutes

Ingredients:

- 2 tablespoons Garlic Oil, plus more as needed
- 2 russet potatoes, cut into ½-inch cubes
- 3 scallions, green parts only, chopped
- ½ teaspoon sea salt, plus more for seasoning the eggs
- ¼ teaspoon freshly ground black pepper, plus more for seasoning the eggs
- 4 eggs

Directions:

1. In a large skillet over medium-high heat, heat the garlic oil until it shimmers.
2. Add the potatoes. Cook for about 20 minutes, stirring occasionally, until soft and browned.
3. Add the scallions, salt, and pepper. Cook for 1 minute more, stirring frequently. Spoon the potatoes onto two plates.
4. Return the skillet to medium heat. If the pan is dry, add a little more garlic oil and swirl it to coat the skillet (see Tip).
5. Carefully crack the eggs into the skillet and season them with a pinch of salt and pepper. Cook undisturbed for 3 to 4 minutes, until the whites solidify.
6. Turn off the heat and carefully flip the eggs so you do not break the yolk. Leave the eggs in the hot pan for 60 to 90 seconds until the surface is cooked but the yolks remain runny.
7. Serve the potatoes topped with the eggs.

Nutrition Info:

- InfoCalories:401; Total Fat: 23g; Saturated Fat: 5g; Carbohydrates: 36g; Fiber: 6g; Sodium: 608mg; Protein: 15g

Banana Toast

Servings:2

Cooking Time: 5 Minutes

Ingredients:

- 4 gluten-free sandwich bread slices
- 1 ripe banana
- ½ teaspoon ground cinnamon

Directions:

1. Toast the bread to your desired doneness.
2. In a small bowl, mash the banana with the cinnamon and spread it on the toast.

Nutrition Info:

- InfoCalories:102; Total Fat: <1g; Saturated Fat: 0g; Carbohydrates: 23g; Fiber: 2g; Sodium: 123mg; Protein: 2g

Pesto Toasted Sandwich

Servings:1

Cooking Time: 5 Minutes

Ingredients:

- 2 slices bread
- 1 tbsp butter
- 1 tbsp pesto, no garlic or onion
- in the mixture
- 4 cherry tomatoes, halved
- 1 slice mozzarella
- ½ cup chicken breast, cooked
- and cubed

Directions:

1. Place a frying pan over medium heat.
2. Butter the outside of each slice of bread.
3. Mix together the filling ingredients and place onto the bread. Ensure the butter is on the outside of the sandwich when assembling.
4. Place the sandwich in the pan and fry for 3 minutes on each side. The bread should be golden.

Nutrition Info:

- Info555g Calories, 35g Total fat, 15g Saturated fat, 28g Carbohydrates, 3 g Fiber, 33g Protein, 3g Sodium.

Quinoa Breakfast Bowl With Basil "hollandaise" Sauce

Servings:4

Cooking Time: 15 Minutes

Ingredients:

- 1 cup uncooked quinoa
- 12 ounces green beans, trimmed and cut into 1-inch pieces
- 1½ cups water
- ½ teaspoon salt
- Basil "Hollandaise" Sauce (here)

Directions:

1. In a medium saucepan, stir together the quinoa, green beans, water, and salt. Bring to a boil over medium-high heat. Reduce the heat to low, cover, and simmer for about 15 minutes, until the quinoa is tender.
2. To serve, spoon the quinoa mixture into bowls and drizzle the sauce over the top.

Nutrition Info:

- InfoCalories: 415; Protein: 9g; Total Fat: 28g; Saturated Fat: 3g; Carbohydrates: 36g; Fiber: 6g; Sodium: 605mg;

Crispy Rice Balls With Parmesan And Corn

Servings:30

Cooking Time:x

Ingredients:

- 3 cups (750 ml) gluten-free, onion-free chicken or vegetable stock*
- ¾ cup (150 g) long-grain white or brown rice
- ¾ cup (2 ounces/60 g) grated Parmesan
- ¾ cup (150 g) canned corn kernels, drained
- 1 large egg, beaten
- 1⅓ cups (160 g) dried gluten-free, soy-free bread crumbs*
- Canola oil, for pan-frying

Directions:

1. Pour the stock into a large saucepan and bring to a boil. Add the rice and cook until tender, 10 to 12 minutes for white rice, 45 to 50 minutes for brown. Drain and return to the pan. While the rice is still warm, stir in the Parmesan and corn. Transfer to a bowl and set aside to cool to room temperature.
2. Preheat the oven to 300°F (150°C).
3. Roll the cooled rice mixture into about 30 golf ball–size balls. Dip the balls in the beaten egg, then roll in the bread crumbs until well coated.
4. Heat a little canola oil in a medium frying pan over medium-high heat. Working in batches of 10, add the rice balls to the pan and cook, turning regularly, until nicely browned all over. Set aside on a baking sheet and keep warm in the oven while you make the rest, adding more oil if needed. Serve warm.

Nutrition Info:

- Info: 45 calories,2 g protein,1 g total fat,7 g carbohydrates,66 mg sodiu.

Blueberry Pancakes

Servings:4
Cooking Time:x
Ingredients:

- 2 large eggs
- 1½ cups (375 ml) low-fat milk, lactose-free milk, or suitable plant-based milk
- 1 cup (130 g) superfine white rice flour
- ½ cup (75 g) cornstarch
- ½ cup (45 g) soy flour
- ⅔ cup (150 g) packed light brown sugar
- 1 tablespoon plus 1 teaspoon gluten-free baking powder
- 1 teaspoon xanthan gum or guar gum
- 4 tablespoons (½ stick/60 g) salted butter, melted
- Nonstick cooking spray
- 1 cup (150 g) fresh or frozen blueberries
- Maple syrup and/or whipped cream, for serving (optional)

Directions:

1. Whisk together the eggs and milk in a small bowl or liquid measuring cup.
2. Sift the rice flour, cornstarch, soy flour, brown sugar, baking powder, and xanthan gum three times into a large bowl (or whisk in the bowl until well combined). Make a well in the center and gradually pour in the milk mixture, mixing well to make a smooth batter. Stir in the melted butter, cover, and set aside for 15 minutes.
3. Heat a large nonstick frying pan or griddle over medium heat and spray with cooking spray. Working in batches, pour in enough batter to form 4-inch (10 cm) pancakes (about ½ cup/125 ml each) and cook for 1 minute or until they start to set. Sprinkle 8 blueberries onto each pancake and cook for 2 minutes more. Turn and cook for 2 minutes or until cooked through. Transfer to a plate and cover loosely with foil to keep warm. Repeat with the remaining batter and berries to make 12 pancakes in total.
4. Sprinkle with the remaining blueberries and serve immediately with maple syrup (if desired) and/or whipped cream for an especially decadent treat.

Nutrition Info:

- Info: 385 calories,9 g protein,12 g total fat,61 g carbohydrates,396 mg sodiu.

Blueberry, Kiwi, And Mint

Servings:1
Cooking Time: 3 Minutes
Ingredients:

- ½ cup blueberries, frozen
- 1 kiwi, small, peeled
- ⅓ cup Greek yogurt
- ⅓ cup water
- 6 mint leaves, fresh

Directions:

1. Mix the ingredients in a blender until creamy.

Nutrition Info:

- Info226g Calories, 12g Total fat, 7g Saturated fat, 27g Carbohydrates, 4 g Fiber, 6g Protein, 19g Sodium.

Easy Breakfast Sausage

Servings:4
Cooking Time: 8 Minutes
Ingredients:

- 1 pound ground pork
- 1 teaspoon ground sage
- ½ teaspoon sea salt
- ⅛ teaspoon red pepper flakes
- ⅛ teaspoon freshly ground black pepper
- Nonstick cooking spray

Directions:

1. In a large bowl, mix the pork, sage, salt, red pepper flakes, and pepper. Form the mixture into 8 patties.
2. Spray a large nonstick skillet with cooking spray and place it over medium-high heat.
3. Add the sausage patties and cook for about 4 minutes per side, until browned on both sides.

Nutrition Info:

- InfoCalories:163; Total Fat: 4g; Saturated Fat: 1g; Carbohydrates: <1g; Fiber: 0g; Sodium: 299mg; Protein: 30g

Basil Omelet With Smashed Tomato

Servings: 2
Cooking Time: 10 Minutes
Ingredients:

- 2 tomatoes, halved
- 3 eggs
- 1 tbsp chives, chopped
- ¼ cup shredded mozzarella cheese (or other FODMAP-approved cheese)
- 1-2 basil leaves, chopped finely
- Pepper

Directions:

1. Break the eggs into a bowl and add a splash of water. Whisk the mixture with a fork and add the chives and a pinch of pepper. Set aside.
2. Place the halved tomatoes on tinfoil in a hot skillet on the stove or onto a hot grill on low to medium heat. Turn occasionally until they are starting to char, then remove them and place them on plates. Squish slightly so that the juices are released.
3. Take the egg mixture and whisk it slightly before pouring it into a hot pan on medium heat. Leave the mixture for a few seconds before gently stirring the uncooked egg until it is cooked but still slightly loose.
4. Place the cheese and a basil leaf on one half of the egg and then gently fold the omelet in half. Let it cook for another minute. Once it is cooked, cut the omelet in half and serve with the tomato.

Nutrition Info:

- Info175.5g Calories, 10.5g Total fat, 48g Saturated fat, 6g Carbohydrates, 1.5 g Fiber, 14.5g Protein, 4g Sodium.

Hawaiian Toasted Sandwich

Servings: 1
Cooking Time: 6 Minutes
Ingredients:

- 2 slices bread
- 1 tbsp butter
- 2 ½ tbsp pineapple chunks, drained
- 2 slices cheddar cheese
- 2 slices ham, cold cut
- 1 tbsp spring onion, tips finely chopped
- Pinch of black pepper

Directions:

1. Place a frying pan over medium heat.
2. Spread butter on the outside of each slice of bread.
3. Prepare the filling by grating the cheese, slicing the ham, rinsing the pineapple, and chopping the spring onion finely.
4. Put the sandwich together adding pepper to taste and ensuring the butter is on the outside.
5. Place in the frying pan and cook each side for 3 minutes. The bread should turn golden brown.
6. Serve warm.

Nutrition Info:

- Info454g Calories, 26.5g Total fat, 9.9g Saturated fat, 33.7g Carbohydrates, 1.8 g Fiber, 19.9g Protein, 3g Sodium.

Overnight Carrot Cake Oats And Walnuts

Servings: 2
Cooking Time: x
Ingredients:

- 3 ounces lactose-free plain yogurt
- ¼ cup unsweetened almond milk
- ½ cup gluten-free rolled oats
- 1 tablespoon chia seeds
- ¼ cup peeled and shredded carrots
- 2 tablespoons crushed pineapple
- ¼ teaspoon alcohol-free vanilla extract
- ½ tablespoon maple syrup
- ½ teaspoon ground cinnamon
- 1 tablespoon walnut halves

Directions:

1. In a medium bowl, combine yogurt, almond milk, and oats; stir. Add chia seeds, carrots, pineapple, vanilla, maple syrup, and cinnamon and stir to combine. Place in 2 small canning jars and cover with lids. Refrigerate overnight.
2. In the morning top with walnuts and enjoy! Can be stored in refrigerator up to 3 days.

Nutrition Info:

- InfoCalories: 342,Fat: 11g,Protein: 7g,Sodium: 44mg,Carbohydrates: 60.

Eggplant Bacon

Servings:4
Cooking Time: 10 Minutes
Ingredients:

- ¼ cup gluten-free soy sauce
- ¼ cup rice vinegar
- 2 tablespoons plus 2 teaspoons olive oil, divided
- 2 tablespoons maple syrup
- 2 teaspoons liquid smoke
- 1 medium eggplant, sliced lengthwise into ¼-inch slabs

Directions:

1. In a medium bowl, combine the soy sauce, vinegar, 2 tablespoons of the olive oil, maple syrup, and liquid smoke.
2. Add the eggplant, toss to coat, and let marinate for 30 minutes, tossing occasionally.
3. Heat the remaining 2 teaspoons of olive oil in a large skillet over medium-high heat. Drain the eggplant slices, reserving the marinade, and cook in a single layer, in batches if needed, for about 5 minutes, until browned on the bottom. Add half of the reserved marinade to the pan (or one-quarter if you are cooking the eggplant in two batches) and cook for another minute, until the liquid has evaporated. Turn the eggplant slices over and cook for another 5 minutes or so, until the second side is browned. Add the remaining marinade (or half of the remaining marinade if cooking two batches) and cook until the liquid has evaporated, for another minute.

Nutrition Info:

- InfoCalories: 151; Protein: 1g; Total Fat: 10g; Saturated Fat: 1g; Carbohydrates: 15g; Fiber: 5g; Sodium: 52mg;

Mediterranean Crustless Quiche

Servings:6
Cooking Time:x
Ingredients:

- 2 teaspoons olive oil
- 2 tomatoes, chopped
- 1 tablespoon balsamic vinegar
- 1 large zucchini, thinly sliced into ribbons
- 1 cup (4 ounces/120 g) grated cheddar
- ½ cup (1½ ounces/40 g) grated Parmesan
- 6 large eggs, lightly beaten
- 3 tablespoons basil leaves
- Salt and freshly ground black pepper

Directions:

1. Preheat the oven to 350°F (170°C). Grease a 9-inch quiche dish or pie pan and line with a parchment paper circle.
2. Heat the olive oil in a nonstick frying pan over medium heat. Add the tomatoes and vinegar and cook until softened.
3. Transfer the tomatoes to a large bowl. Add the zucchini, cheddar, Parmesan, eggs, basil, and salt and pepper and mix to combine. Pour the quiche into the baking dish.
4. Bake for 20 to 25 minutes, until firm and lightly golden. Let stand for 5 minutes before slicing.

Nutrition Info:

- Info: 215 calories,15 g protein,15 g total fat,5 g carbohydrates,415 mg sodiu.

Cheesy Corn Muffins

Servings:1
Cooking Time:x
Ingredients:

- ½ cup (75 g) cornstarch
- ½ cup (65 g) tapioca flour
- 2 teaspoons gluten-free baking powder
- 1 teaspoon baking soda
- 1 teaspoon xanthan gum or guar gum
- 3 tablespoons (45 g) salted butter, melted
- ¾ cup (200 g) gluten-free low-fat plain yogurt
- 3 large eggs
- ½ cup (2 ounces/60 g) grated cheddar, plus twelve ⅓-inch (1 cm) cubes
- ½ cup (1½ ounces/40 g) finely grated Parmesan
- 4 to 6 lean bacon slices (4 ounces/115 g), cooked until crispy (see directions under Bacon and Zucchini Crustless Quiche) and crumbled (optional)
- 1 cup (200 g) drained canned or thawed frozen corn kernels
- Pinch of salt and freshly ground black pepper

Directions:
1. Preheat the oven to 325°F (170°C) and line a 12-cup muffin pan with paper liners.
2. Sift the rice flour, cornstarch, tapioca flour, baking powder, baking soda, and xanthan gum three times into a large bowl (or whisk in the bowl until well combined).
3. Combine the melted butter, yogurt, eggs, cheddar, Parmesan, bacon (if using), and corn in a medium bowl. Add the yogurt mixture to the flour mixture and stir with a large metal spoon until just combined (do not overmix). Season with salt and pepper. Half-fill the muffin cups with the batter, then place a cube of cheddar in each one. Pour in the remaining batter until the cups are two-thirds full.
4. Bake for 15 to 20 minutes, until firm to the touch and a toothpick inserted into the center of a muffin (avoid the cheese filling) comes out clean. Cool in the pan for 5 minutes, then turn out onto a wire rack to cool completely.

Nutrition Info:
- Info: 218 calories,9 g protein,11 g total fat,21 g carbohydrates,546 mg sodiu.

Pumpkin Pie Pancakes

Servings:4
Cooking Time: 10 Minutes
Ingredients:

- 1 cup pumpkin purée
- 4 eggs, beaten
- 1 tablespoon ground flaxseed
- 1 tablespoon buckwheat flour
- 1 teaspoon baking powder
- 1 teaspoon pumpkin pie spice
- Pinch sea salt
- Nonstick cooking spray

Directions:
1. In a small bowl, whisk the pumpkin purée and eggs until well mixed.
2. In a medium bowl, whisk the flaxseed, buckwheat flour, baking powder, pumpkin pie spice, and salt.
3. Fold the wet ingredients into the dry ingredients until combined.
4. Spray a large nonstick skillet with cooking spray and place it over medium-high heat.
5. Spoon the batter in scant ¼-cup amounts onto the heated skillet. With the back of a spoon, spread the batter thin. Cook for about 3 minutes, until bubbles form on the top. Flip and cook for about 3 minutes more, until browned on the other side.

Nutrition Info:
- InfoCalories:102; Total Fat: 5g; Saturated Fat: 2g; Carbohydrates: 8g; Fiber: 3g; Sodium: 105mg; Protein: 7g

Fish And Seafood Recipes

Salmon Noodle Casserole

Servings:8
Cooking Time:x
Ingredients:

- 3 small sweet potatoes
- 1 pound gluten-free egg noodles
- 1/4 cup Sweet Barbecue Sauce (see recipe in Chapter 9)
- 1 (5-ounce) can salmon, drained and flaked with a fork
- 1 cup freshly grated Parmesan cheese, divided
- 2 slices gluten-free bread, toasted
- 1/2 cup shelled pecans
- 1 teaspoon sea salt, divided
- 1/2 teaspoon freshly ground pepper, divided
- 3/4 cup lactose-free whole milk
- 1/4 cup lactose-free plain low-fat yogurt
- 1 cup Vegetable Stock (see recipe in Chapter 8)
- 1 cup shredded fontina cheese
- 1 cup packed baby spinach leaves

Directions:

1. Preheat oven to 400°F. Poke a few holes in each sweet potato and place in a small baking dish. Bake sweet potatoes for 45 minutes. Remove from oven, slice open to cool, and set aside.
2. Cook noodles according to package directions to an al dente texture.
3. Heat barbecue sauce in a small skillet over medium heat. Add salmon and sauté very carefully for about 3 minutes until fully coated. Remove from heat.
4. In a food processor, add 1/2 cup Parmesan cheese, toast, pecans, 1/2 teaspoon salt, and 1/4 teaspoon pepper. Pulse to a bread-crumb consistency. Transfer to a medium bowl.
5. Once cool enough to handle, scoop inside flesh from sweet potatoes and transfer to food processor. Add milk, yogurt, stock, and remaining salt and pepper and process to combine.
6. Add fontina and remaining 1/2 cup Parmesan cheese and pulse until combined.
7. Transfer noodles to a 13" × 9" baking dish. Pour sweet potato mixture over noodles and stir to combine.
8. Tuck spinach leaves between the noodles. Dot top of casserole evenly with salmon mixture.
9. Sprinkle top of casserole evenly with bread-crumb mixture. Bake 20 minutes, or until cheese is melted and bubbling or browning. Let sit for 5 minutes, then serve.

Nutrition Info:

- InfoCalories: 510,Fat: 19g,Protein: 25g,Sodium: 1,140mg,Carbohydrates: 61.

Glazed Salmon

Servings:4
Cooking Time:x
Ingredients:

- 1/4 cup gluten-free tamari
- 1 tablespoon almond butter
- 1 tablespoon pure maple syrup
- 2 teaspoons rice vinegar
- 2 teaspoons sesame oil
- 1 teaspoon blackstrap molasses
- 1/8 teaspoon ground ginger
- 12-ounce fillet of salmon

Directions:

1. Make glaze: Mix all ingredients except salmon in a small saucepan.
2. Transfer 2 tablespoons glaze to a small bowl.
3. Heat a charcoal grill, gas grill, or broiler to 350ºF. Grill or broil salmon, skin-side down, for 15 minutes, basting with the sauce in the small bowl.
4. While salmon is cooking, heat remaining glaze over medium-low heat for about 5 minutes to thicken.
5. When salmon is fully cooked, remove from heat, drizzle with heated glaze, and serve.

Nutrition Info:

- InfoCalories: 190,Fat: 10g,Protein: 19g,Sodium: 955mg,Carbohydrates: 6.

Shrimp And Cheese Casserole

Servings:4
Cooking Time:x

Ingredients:

- 3 tablespoons butter
- 1/8 teaspoon salt
- 1/8 teaspoon freshly ground black pepper
- 1/8 teaspoon wheat-free asafetida powder
- 1/4 cup dry white wine
- 10 ounces fresh spinach, chopped
- 1 (14.5-ounce) can diced tomatoes, drained
- 10 ounces medium shrimp, peeled and deveined
- 2 tablespoons olive oil
- 1/4 pound crumbled feta cheese
- 1/4 pound shredded mozzarella cheese

Directions:

1. Preheat oven to 350°F. Grease a 9" × 13"casserole dish.
2. In a large skillet, melt butter over medium-high heat; add salt, pepper, and asafetida and stir.
3. Add wine and spinach and cook 2–3 minutes.
4. Put spinach mixture into prepared casserole dish and layer in diced tomatoes. Place shrimp on top, drizzle with olive oil. Sprinkle with feta and mozzarella.
5. Bake 25 minutes or until cheese is bubbly and slightly brown.

Nutrition Info:

- InfoCalories: 346,Fat: 22g,Protein: 27g,Sodium: 790mg,Carbohydrates: 8.

Grilled Cod With Fresh Basil

Servings:4
Cooking Time:x

Ingredients:

- 3 tablespoons extra-virgin olive oil
- Juice of 1 medium lemon
- 2 pounds cod fillet
- 1 garlic clove, peeled, slightly smashed
- 8 tablespoons butter (1 stick)
- 2 tablespoons chopped fresh basil
- 1 pinch ground red pepper

Directions:

1. Combine oil and lemon juice in a shallow dish. Add cod and turn to coat. Marinate for 30 minutes at room temperature.
2. Heat a charcoal or gas grill to 350ºF. Grill fish for 15 minutes or until cooked through, flipping once after 8 minutes.
3. When fish is on its second side, put garlic and butter in a small saucepan and cook over low heat for 5 minutes. Turn off heat, remove and discard the garlic, and add basil and ground red pepper.
4. Remove cod from grill and serve with basil sauce on the side.

Nutrition Info:

- InfoCalories: 400,Fat: 25g,Protein: 40g,Sodium: 125mg,Carbohydrates: 1.

Creamy Halibut

Servings:4
Cooking Time:x

Ingredients:

- 2 teaspoons sunflower oil
- 1 1/2 pounds halibut, cut into 4 portions
- 1/3 cup Basic Mayonnaise (see Chapter 13)
- 2 1/2 tablespoons lemon juice
- 2 1/4 tablespoons grated Parmesan cheese
- 1/8 teaspoon wheat-free asafetida powder
- 1 teaspoon Dijon mustard
- 1/2 teaspoon crushed red pepper flakes
- 2 tablespoons chopped fresh flat-leaf parsley

Directions:

1. Preheat oven to 400°F.
2. Heat oil in a large nonstick skillet over medium-high heat. Brown halibut on both sides, about 3 minutes each side.
3. Remove fish from skillet and place in a 9" × 13" ovenproof casserole dish. Bake 7 minutes.
4. While fish is baking, mix together remaining ingredients except parsley in a medium bowl.
5. Once fish is done baking, spoon mixture over fish and broil in oven 2 minutes. Garnish with parsley.

Nutrition Info:

- InfoCalories: 358,Fat: 22g,Protein: 37g,Sodium: 267mg,Carbohydrates: 2.

Summery Fish Stew

Servings:6
Cooking Time:x
Ingredients:

- 2 slices raw bacon
- 1 cup sliced carrot
- 4 cups Seafood Stock (see recipe in Chapter 8)
- 1/2 cup dry white wine
- 1 (14.5-ounce) can fire-roasted diced tomatoes
- 1 bay leaf
- 1 teaspoon sea salt
- 1/4 teaspoon freshly ground black pepper
- 2 small red potatoes, peeled and cut into 1" pieces
- 2 pounds raw white-fleshed fish fillets, cut into 2" pieces
- 1 cup cut green beans
- 1 cup corn kernels
- 1/2 cup Whipped Cream (see recipe in Chapter 14)
- 1 tablespoon chopped fresh parsley

Directions:

1. Cook bacon in a large stockpot over medium heat. Transfer bacon to a paper towel–lined plate to cool.
2. To same pot, add carrots and sauté for 10 minutes over medium-low heat, stirring occasionally. Add stock, wine, tomatoes, bay leaf, salt, and pepper.
3. Bring just to a boil, then reduce heat and simmer for 20 minutes. Add potatoes and simmer uncovered 15 minutes. Add fish, beans, and corn; return to a simmer, stirring occasionally. Simmer uncovered 5 minutes. Remove from heat and let stand 5 minutes more, until fish is cooked through.
4. Remove and discard bay leaf. Chop and add in bacon. Stir in whipped cream.
5. Ladle stew into bowls, garnish with parsley, and serve.

Nutrition Info:

- InfoCalories: 414,Fat: 15g,Protein: 36g,Sodium: 1,455mg,Carbohydrates: 31.

Baked Moroccan-style Halibut

Servings:4
Cooking Time:x
Ingredients:

- 1 pint cherry tomatoes
- 1/4 cup pitted black olives
- 1/8 teaspoon wheat-free asafetida powder
- 1/2 teaspoon ground cumin
- 1/4 teaspoon ground cinnamon
- 1/4 teaspoon freshly ground black pepper
- 4 (6-ounce) fresh halibut fillets
- 2 tablespoons olive oil

Directions:

1. Preheat oven 450°F.
2. In a medium mixing bowl, stir together tomatoes, olives, asafetida, cumin, cinnamon, and black pepper.
3. Add halibut to a large baking dish. Sprinkle tomato mixture evenly over fish. Drizzle oil over fish.
4. Bake 10–15 minutes or until an instant-read thermometer inserted into the thickest fillet reads 145°F. Serve immediately.

Nutrition Info:

- InfoCalories: 269,Fat: 12g,Protein: 36g,Sodium: 168mg,Carbohydrates: 4.

Sole Meunière

Servings:2
Cooking Time:x
Ingredients:

- 2 (4-ounce) boneless, skinless sole fillets
- ¼ teaspoon kosher salt
- ¼ teaspoon freshly ground black pepper
- ¼ cup gluten-free all-purpose flour
- 4 tablespoons unsalted butter, divided
- 1½ tablespoons finely chopped fresh flat-leaf parsley
- ½ teaspoon grated lemon zest
- Pulp ½ large lemon, seeds removed

Directions:

1. Season fillets on both sides with salt and pepper and lay on a plate. Place flour in a shallow bowl. Dredge fillets in flour, shaking off any excess.
2. Heat 2 tablespoons butter in a 12" skillet over medium-high heat. Place fillets in skillet and cook until browned on both sides and just cooked through, about 6 minutes.
3. Transfer fillets to plates; sprinkle with parsley.
4. Using a paper towel, carefully wipe skillet clean and return to heat. Add remaining butter, stir, and cook until it starts to brown. Add lemon zest and pulp; cook 3–4 minutes, then pour over fillets. Serve immediately.

Nutrition Info:

- InfoCalories: 364,Fat: 25g,Protein: 23g,Sodium: 390mg,Carbohydrates: 12.

Mediterranean Flaky Fish With Vegetables

Servings:4
Cooking Time:x
Ingredients:

- 4 (3.5-ounce) skinless Atlantic cod fillets
- 1 cup grated zucchini
- ¼ cup thinly sliced fresh basil, plus 4 whole basil leaves
- 20 cherry tomatoes, halved
- 10 black olives, sliced
- ¼ teaspoon kosher salt
- ½ teaspoon freshly ground black pepper
- 4 tablespoons dry white wine, divided
- 4 tablespoons extra-virgin olive oil, divided

Directions:

1. Preheat oven to 400°F.
2. Make parchment pockets: Pull out a 17" × 11" piece of parchment paper. With one longer edge closest to you, fold in half from left to right. Using scissors, cut out a large heart shape. On a large cutting board or clean work surface, lay down parchment heart and place fish on one half of heart, leaving at least a 1½" border around fillet. Repeat with remaining fish fillets. Lay parchment hearts in a 9" × 13" baking dish.
3. In a medium bowl, combine zucchini, sliced basil, tomatoes, olives, salt, and pepper. Stir to combine.
4. Evenly distribute the vegetables over each fish fillet in the parchment hearts.
5. Take opposite side of each parchment heart and fold over, making both edges of heart line up. Starting at rounded end, crimp edges together tightly. Leave a few inches at pointed end unfolded. Grab pointed edge and tilt heart to pour in 1 tablespoon each of wine and oil. Finish by crimping edges and twisting pointed end around and under packet.
6. Bake until just cooked through, about 10–12 minutes. Poke a toothpick through parchment paper. Fish should be done if toothpick easily slides through fish. Carefully cut open packets (steam will escape). Garnish with whole basil leaves.

Nutrition Info:

- InfoCalories: 246,Fat: 16g,Protein: 19g,Sodium: 304mg,Carbohydrates: 6.

Shrimp With Cherry Tomatoes

Servings:4
Cooking Time:x
Ingredients:

- 1 pound gluten-free spaghetti
- 2 medium zucchini, trimmed
- 1 pound carrots, peeled
- 3 tablespoons extra-virgin olive oil, divided
- 1 pint cherry tomatoes, halved
- 3 tablespoons butter
- 3 tablespoons white wine
- Juice of 1 medium lemon
- 2 tablespoons chopped fresh basil
- 2 cloves garlic, peeled and slightly crushed
- 1 1/2 pounds peeled and deveined shrimp
- 1/8 teaspoon sea salt
- 1/8 teaspoon freshly ground black pepper

Directions:

1. Cook spaghetti according to package directions.
2. With vegetable peeler, peel zucchini and carrots into long strips. Heat 1 tablespoon of oil in a large skillet over medium heat. Add vegetables and sauté until soft, approximately 5–8 minutes, stirring frequently. Transfer to a bowl and keep warm. Wipe the skillet clean with a paper towel.
3. In a medium skillet, combine tomatoes, butter, wine, lemon juice, and basil. Cook over low heat for 10 minutes, stirring occasionally, then keep warm.
4. While tomatoes are cooking, heat the remaining 2 tablespoons of oil in the large skillet over medium heat. Add garlic and sauté until just starting to brown, about 5 minutes. Remove garlic and add shrimp to oil. Sauté shrimp until cooked through, approximately 8 minutes, stirring frequently. Season with salt and pepper.
5. To serve, place spaghetti on a serving platter and top with vegetable mixture, shrimp, and tomato mixture.

Nutrition Info:

- InfoCalories: 848,Fat: 24g,Protein: 52g,Sodium: 420mg,Carbohydrates: 103.

Shrimp Puttanesca With Linguine

Servings:4
Cooking Time:x
Ingredients:

- 1 pound gluten-free linguine
- 2 tablespoons olive oil
- 1 (24-ounce) can diced tomatoes
- 2 cups shredded kale
- 1/2 cup black olives
- 1/2 cup green olives
- 2 tablespoons capers, rinsed and drained
- 1 teaspoon red pepper flakes
- 1 pound large shrimp
- 1/2 cup crumbled feta cheese

Directions:

1. Cook pasta according to package directions. Drain and set aside.
2. Heat oil in a large skillet over medium heat. Stir in tomatoes, kale, black and green olives, capers, and red pepper flakes. Bring to a boil, then reduce heat to a simmer and cook 15 minutes.
3. Add pasta, shrimp, and cheese to sauce. Cook 3–5 minutes or until shrimp is cooked through.

Nutrition Info:

- InfoCalories: 529,Fat: 18g,Protein: 42g,Sodium: 1,130mg,Carbohydrates: 98.

Coconut Shrimp

Servings:4
Cooking Time:x
Ingredients:

- 1 slice gluten-free bread, toasted
- 1⁄2 cup unsweetened finely shredded coconut
- 1⁄8 teaspoon sea salt
- 1 large egg
- 1⁄8 teaspoon pure vanilla extract
- 16 large raw shrimp, peeled and deveined

Directions:

1. Preheat oven to 425°F. Line a baking sheet with foil and coat with coconut oil spray.
2. Add toast to food processor. Pulse until fine bread crumbs form.
3. In a flat dish, mix bread crumbs with coconut and salt.
4. In a small bowl, whisk together egg and vanilla.
5. Dip each shrimp into egg mixture, then into bread-crumb/coconut mixture. Transfer to baking sheet.
6. Bake for 5 minutes. Carefully turn each shrimp over and bake for 5 minutes more or until shrimp are fully cooked through. Serve immediately.

Nutrition Info:

- InfoCalories: 88,Fat: 5g,Protein: 5g,Sodium: 160mg,Carbohydrates: 6.

Basic Baked Scallops

Servings:2
Cooking Time:x
Ingredients:

- 3⁄4 pound sea scallops
- 2 tablespoons lemon juice
- 21⁄2 tablespoons unsalted butter, melted
- 1⁄4 teaspoon sea salt
- 1⁄2 teaspoon freshly ground black pepper
- 2 tablespoons chopped fresh flat-leaf parsley
- 1⁄2 cup gluten-free bread crumbs
- 1⁄2 teaspoon smoked paprika
- 2 tablespoons olive oil

Directions:

1. Preheat oven to 425°F.
2. Toss together scallops, lemon juice, melted butter, salt, and pepper in a 2-quart baking dish.
3. In a medium bowl, combine parsley, bread crumbs, paprika, and olive oil. Sprinkle on top of scallops.
4. Bake 12–14 minutes or until scallops are heated through and bread crumbs are golden. Serve immediately.

Nutrition Info:

- InfoCalories: 426,Fat: 30g,Protein: 17g,Sodium: 621mg,Carbohydrates: 23.

Light Tuna Casserole

Servings:8
Cooking Time:x
Ingredients:

- 1 tablespoon butter
- 2 large carrots, peeled and diced
- 1/4 cup gluten-free all-purpose flour
- 1 1/2 cups chicken stock
- 1 1/2 cups lactose-free milk
- 1 cup frozen green beans, thawed
- 1 teaspoon dried oregano
- 1 teaspoon dried marjoram
- 1 teaspoon dried rosemary
- 1 teaspoon dried thyme
- 1/2 teaspoon salt
- 1/4 teaspoon freshly ground black pepper
- 3 (5-ounce) cans tuna in water, drained
- 8 ounces gluten-free egg noodles, cooked al dente
- 1/2 cup shredded sharp Cheddar cheese
- 1/2 cup shredded Colby cheese
- 2 tablespoons gluten-free panko bread crumbs

Directions:

1. Preheat oven to 400°F.
2. Melt butter in a large saucepan over medium-high heat. Add carrots, and sauté 5–7 minutes, or until soft. Stir in flour and cook 1 minute.
3. Whisk in stock, then stir in milk, green beans, oregano, marjoram, rosemary, thyme, salt, pepper, and tuna. Continue cooking, stirring occasionally, about 5 minutes.
4. Add sauce mixture to noodles and toss to combine. Stir in Cheddar and Colby cheese.
5. Pour noodles into a greased 9" × 13" baking pan. Sprinkle bread crumbs on top. Bake 18–20 minutes or until top is crispy and golden and filling is bubbling. Serve immediately.

Nutrition Info:

- InfoCalories: 339,Fat: 11g,Protein: 23g,Sodium: 650mg,Carbohydrates: 35.

Tilapia Piccata

Servings:6
Cooking Time:x
Ingredients:

- 1/4 cup dry white wine
- 3 tablespoons freshly squeezed lemon juice, preferably Meyer
- 1 teaspoon fresh lemon zest
- 2 tablespoons capers, rinsed, drained
- 1/4 cup sweet rice flour, divided
- 1/2 teaspoon sea salt
- 1/4 teaspoon freshly ground black pepper
- 4 (6-ounce) pieces tilapia fillets
- 1 tablespoon Garlic-Infused Oil (see recipe in Chapter 9)
- 1 teaspoon butter
- 1 tablespoon chopped fresh parsley

Directions:

1. In a small bowl, whisk wine, lemon juice, zest, and capers.
2. Reserve 1 teaspoon flour and set aside. Mix remaining flour with salt and pepper on a plate. Dip fish into flour.
3. Heat oil over medium heat in a large skillet. Add fish and cook 2–3 minutes per side. When fish is cooked through, remove from pan.
4. Add wine mixture and reserved flour to pan and cook 1 minute, whisking constantly. Remove from heat and stir in butter.
5. Top fish with the sauce, garnish with parsley, and serve immediately.

Nutrition Info:

- InfoCalories: 168,Fat: 5g,Protein: 23g,Sodium: 342mg,Carbohydrates: 6.

Atlantic Cod With Basil Walnut Sauce

Servings:4
Cooking Time:x
Ingredients:

- 2 (6-ounce) Atlantic cod fillets
- 1/4 teaspoon kosher salt, divided
- 1/2 teaspoon freshly ground black pepper, divided
- Zest of 1 large lemon
- 3 tablespoons extra-virgin olive oil, divided
- 1/4 packed cup fresh basil leaves
- 1 tablespoon small walnut pieces

Directions:

1. Preheat oven to 400°F.
2. Place fish fillets in a 9″ x 13″ baking dish and sprinkle 1/8 teaspoon salt, 1/4 teaspoon pepper, and lemon zest over both sides of fish. Brush with 1 tablespoon olive oil.
3. Using a food processor, combine basil, walnuts, 1/8 teaspoon salt, and 1/4 teaspoon pepper. Process until it becomes a paste. With processor running, gradually add 2 tablespoons olive oil. Pat mixture evenly over fish.
4. Place baking dish in oven and bake for 13–17 minutes or until flesh is opaque in color. Serve with rice, spooning the juices from the pan over the fish and rice.

Nutrition Info:

- InfoCalories: 176,Fat: 12g,Protein: 16g,Sodium: 194mg,Carbohydrates:2.

Seafood Risotto

Servings:6
Cooking Time:x
Ingredients:

- 21/2 cups water
- 2 (8-ounce) bottles clam juice
- 6 tablespoons olive oil, divided
- 11/2 cups arborio rice
- 1/2 cup dry white wine
- 3/4 pound uncooked large shrimp, peeled, deveined, coarsely chopped
- 3/4 pound bay scallops
- 1/8 teaspoon wheat-free asafetida powder
- 1 tablespoon butter
- 1/2 cup grated Parmesan cheese
- 2 tablespoons finely chopped fresh Italian parsley

Directions:

1. Combine water and clam juice in a medium saucepan. Bring to simmer. Keep warm over low heat.
2. Heat 3 tablespoons oil in heavy, large saucepan over medium heat. Add rice; sauté 2 minutes.
3. Add wine; stir until liquid is absorbed, about 2 minutes. Add 1 cup clam juice mixture to rice. Simmer until liquid is absorbed, stirring often. Continue adding clam juice mixture 1/2 cup at a time, stirring often and simmering until liquid is absorbed before each addition. Simmer until rice is tender but still slightly firm in center and mixture is creamy, about 25 minutes.
4. Heat remaining 3 tablespoons oil in a separate heavy, large skillet over medium-high heat. Add shrimp, scallops, and asafetida. Sauté until shrimp and scallops are opaque in center, about 6 minutes.
5. Add seafood to rice. Stir and add butter; cook 4 minutes longer. Remove from heat and stir in Parmesan cheese. Transfer to serving bowl.
6. Garnish with chopped parsley and serve.

Nutrition Info:

- InfoCalories: 514,Fat: 22g,Protein: 30g,Sodium: 478mg,Carbohydrates: 43.

Rita's Linguine With Clam Sauce

Servings:4
Cooking Time:x
Ingredients:

- 12 ounces gluten-free linguine
- 1 tablespoon olive oil
- 1 tablespoon garlic-infused olive oil
- 1/8 teaspoon wheat-free asafetida powder
- 2 tablespoons unsalted butter, divided
- 1/2 cup dry white wine
- 1 teaspoon dried oregano
- 2 dozen cherrystone clams, rinsed and scrubbed
- 1/4 cup coarsely chopped fresh flat-leaf parsley
- 1/2 teaspoon freshly ground black pepper

Directions:

1. Cook pasta until al dente according to package directions. Reserve 1/2 cup pasta water; drain pasta. Set aside.
2. While pasta cooks, heat oils over medium heat in a 5-quart saucepan. Add asafetida, 1 tablespoon butter, wine, and oregano and bring to a boil; cook 2 minutes.
3. Add clams; cover and simmer until clams open, about 10 minutes. If any clams have not opened, discard.
4. Add pasta to clams and stir 1 minute. Remove from heat and stir in 1 tablespoon butter, parsley, black pepper, and reserved pasta water; stir to combine. Serve immediately.

Nutrition Info:

- InfoCalories: 456,Fat: 14g,Protein: 12g,Sodium: 14mg,Carbohydrates: 65.

Grilled Swordfish With Pineapple Salsa

Servings:4
Cooking Time:x
Ingredients:

- 2 tablespoons finely chopped cilantro
- 2 medium limes, juiced and zested
- 1 medium orange, juiced and zested
- 1/2 whole pineapple, cut into small chunks
- 1/4 teaspoon kosher salt
- 1/2 teaspoon freshly ground black pepper
- 4 (3.5-ounce) swordfish steaks, 1" thick
- 2 tablespoons olive oil

Directions:

1. In a medium bowl, combine cilantro, lime and orange juice and zest, and pineapple; set aside.
2. Set a gas grill to medium-high or heat a cast-iron skillet over medium-high heat. Mix salt and pepper together in a small bowl.
3. Brush swordfish with oil and sprinkle with salt and pepper.
4. Cook fish 5 minutes on one side and 3 minutes on other side.
5. Transfer swordfish to plates; top with pineapple salsa.

Nutrition Info:

- InfoCalories: 267,Fat: 11g,Protein: 20g,Sodium: 238mg,Carbohydrates: 24.

Cedar Planked Salmon

Servings:4
Cooking Time:x
Ingredients:

- Cedar grilling plank
- 1 tablespoon demerara sugar
- 1 teaspoon freshly ground tricolored peppercorns
- 1/4 teaspoon sea salt
- 1/8 teaspoon pure vanilla extract
- 12-ounce raw salmon fillet

Directions:

1. Prepare cedar plank by soaking in warm water for at least 1 hour.
2. In a small bowl, mix sugar, peppercorns, salt, and vanilla. Rub all over salmon and transfer, skin-side down, to prepared plank.
3. Heat a charcoal grill, gas grill, or broiler to 350°F. Grill or broil salmon, skin-side down on plank, for 15 minutes.

Nutrition Info:

- InfoCalories: 133,Fat: 5g,Protein: 17g,Sodium: 185mg,Carbohydrates: 4.

Grilled Halibut With Lemony Pesto

Servings:4
Cooking Time:x
Ingredients:

- 1 tablespoon grapeseed oil
- 2 tablespoons freshly squeezed lemon juice, divided
- 2 teaspoons grated lemon zest, divided
- 1⁄2 teaspoon sea salt
- 1⁄4 teaspoon freshly ground black pepper
- 4 (6-ounce) raw halibut steaks
- 1⁄2 cup Garden Pesto (see recipe in Chapter 9)

Directions:

1. Whisk oil, 1 tablespoon lemon juice, 1 teaspoon zest, salt, and pepper in a large bowl. Add halibut and marinate for 30 minutes.
2. Add pesto, remaining juice, and remaining zest to a food processor. Pulse just until combined.
3. Heat a charcoal grill, gas grill, or broiler to 350°F. Grill or broil steaks, about 6 minutes per side until fish is cooked through.
4. Top fish with the lemony pesto and serve immediately.

Nutrition Info:

- InfoCalories: 356,Fat: 20g,Protein: 39g,Sodium: 675mg,Carbohydrates: 3.

Maple-glazed Salmon

Servings:2
Cooking Time:x
Ingredients:

- 2 tablespoons toasted sesame seeds
- 3 tablespoons maple syrup
- 3 tablespoons sesame oil
- 1⁄4 cup gluten-free soy sauce (tamari)
- 1⁄8 teaspoon freshly ground black pepper
- 1⁄8 teaspoon wheat-free asafetida powder
- 2 (6-ounce) wild salmon fillets
- 1 tablespoon thinly sliced fresh gingerroot
- 2 scallions, chopped, green part only

Directions:

1. To toast sesame seeds, use a small dry skillet and place over medium heat. Toast 3–5 minutes or until lightly browned, stirring occasionally. Set aside on a plate.
2. In a large, shallow dish, whisk maple syrup, sesame oil, tamari, pepper, and asafetida. Once evenly combined, add salmon to mixture and using tongs, turn fish to evenly coat every side. Place ginger slices on top of salmon. Cover and refrigerate at least 2 hours. If possible, refrigerate up to 24 hours so more of the flavors marinate throughout the fish.
3. Preheat oven to 450°F.
4. Remove salmon from refrigerator and using tongs, coat both sides of fish with toasted sesame seeds. Place salmon in a 9" × 13" baking dish and cook 10–12 minutes or until salmon is opaque in center. An instant-read thermometer should register 145°F in thickest part of fillet.
5. Transfer to plates and garnish with scallions.

Nutrition Info:

- InfoCalories: 573,Fat: 35g,Protein: 37g,Sodium: 1,876mg,Carbohydrates: 26.

Citrusy Swordfish Skewers

Servings:4
Cooking Time:x

Ingredients:

- 2 medium oranges, peeled
- 4 (4-ounce) swordfish steaks
- 2 tablespoons Garlic-Infused Oil (see recipe in Chapter 9)
- 1 tablespoon orange juice
- 1 teaspoon dried oregano
- 1/2 teaspoon sea salt

Directions:

1. Cut each orange into six equal parts. Cut swordfish into 2" cubes.
2. Combine oil, orange juice, oregano, and salt in a medium bowl. Whisk marinade; add fish and orange pieces. Toss to coat. Marinate for 60 minutes, tossing occasionally.
3. Skewer the swordfish and orange pieces in an alternating fish/fruit pattern.
4. Heat grill or broiler to medium. Grill or broil skewers for 15 minutes, turning once, until fish is cooked through. Serve immediately.

Nutrition Info:

- InfoCalories: 230,Fat: 11g,Protein: 23g,Sodium: 395mg,Carbohydrates: 9.

Feta Crab Cakes

Servings:4
Cooking Time:x

Ingredients:

- 5 slices gluten-free bread, toasted
- 1/2 teaspoon sea salt
- 1/8 teaspoon freshly ground black pepper
- 12 ounces lump cooked crabmeat
- 1/2 cup crumbled feta cheese
- 1/2 teaspoon dried basil
- 1/2 teaspoon dried oregano
- 1/2 teaspoon dried marjoram
- 1/2 teaspoon dried thyme
- 1 tablespoon lactose-free plain low-fat yogurt
- 1 large egg, beaten, divided

Directions:

1. Preheat oven to 400°F. Line a baking sheet with parchment paper and brush with safflower oil.
2. Add toast, salt, and pepper to a food processor. Pulse until fine bread crumbs form.
3. In a large bowl, combine 1/3 cup bread crumbs, crabmeat, feta, basil, oregano, marjoram, thyme, yogurt, and 1 tablespoon beaten egg. Stir well to combine.
4. Place remaining beaten egg in a bowl. Place remaining bread crumbs in a separate shallow bowl. Create 8 equal round balls of crab mixture. Working with one ball at a time, flatten to a 1/2" disc, then coat in egg, followed by bread crumbs. Transfer to baking sheet.
5. Bake 10 minutes, then carefully turn each cake over and bake 10 minutes more.

Nutrition Info:

- InfoCalories: 270,Fat: 7g,Protein: 26g,Sodium: 1,065mg,Carbohydrates: 24.

Fish And Chips

Servings:4
Cooking Time:x

Ingredients:

- ¼ cup millet
- ¼ cup chopped pecans
- 2 tablespoons cornmeal
- 1½ teaspoons sea salt, divided
- ⅛ teaspoon ground red pepper
- 4 small red potatoes, thinly sliced
- 1 tablespoon extra-virgin olive oil
- ½ cup lactose-free 2% milk
- 2 tablespoons light sour cream
- 12 ounces tilapia fillets

Directions:

1. In a medium bowl, cover millet with boiling water and soak for 30 minutes.
2. Preheat oven to 400°F. Line 2 baking sheets with parchment paper.
3. Drain millet completely and spread on one baking sheet. Add pecans to second baking sheet. Roast millet and pecans for 10 minutes, tossing halfway through.
4. Process pecans in a food processor until finely ground. Transfer to a medium shallow dish; toss with millet, cornmeal, ½ teaspoon salt, and red pepper.
5. Toss potato slices in oil and 1 teaspoon salt. Re-line one baking sheet and scatter it with potatoes. Roast in oven for 30 minutes or until brown and crisp.
6. In another shallow dish, whisk together milk and sour cream.
7. Re-line the second baking sheet and coat with cooking spray. Working with one piece at a time, dip tilapia in milk mixture and then carefully coat both sides in millet mixture. Transfer to baking sheet.
8. Bake for 15 minutes or until fish is cooked through. Serve with the potato chips.

Nutrition Info:

- InfoCalories: 360,Fat: 12g,Protein: 24g,Sodium: 955mg,Carbohydrates: 42.

Meat Recipes

Lime Pork Stir-fry With Rice Noodles

Servings:4
Cooking Time:x
Ingredients:
- 1 heaping tablespoon finely grated ginger
- 6 kaffir lime leaves, shredded, or 1½ heaping tablespoons grated lime zest
- 1 small red chile pepper, seeded and thinly sliced
- 2 tablespoons plus 2 teaspoons fresh lime juice
- ¼ cup (55 g) brown sugar
- ⅓ cup (80 ml) gluten-free soy sauce
- 3 tablespoons sesame oil
- 1 pound 5 ounces (600 g) lean pork, cut into ⅛-inch (3 to 4 mm) strips
- 8 ounces (225 g) rice noodles
- 1 bunch bok choy, leaves separated, cut if large, rinsed, and drained
- 1 red bell pepper, seeded and cut into thin strips
- 1½ cups (150 g) broccoli florets
- ¼ cup (5 g) roughly chopped cilantro

Directions:
1. Combine the ginger, lime leaves, chile pepper, lime juice, brown sugar, 1 tablespoon of the soy sauce, and 1 tablespoon of the sesame oil in a bowl. Add the pork and toss to coat, then cover and refrigerate for 3 to 4 hours or overnight.
2. Shortly before you're ready to eat, soak the noodles in boiling water for 5 minutes or until tender. Drain and set aside until needed.
3. Heat the remaining 2 tablespoons of sesame oil in a wok, add the pork strips and stir-fry until just cooked.
4. Add the bok choy, bell pepper, broccoli, and the remaining soy sauce and cook until the vegetables are just tender.
5. Add the noodles and toss to combine. Sprinkle with the cilantro and serve.

Nutrition Info:
- Info613 calories; 38 g protein; 20 g total fat; 4 g saturated fat; 72 g carbohydrates; 5 g fiber; 1091 mg sodium

Fish And Potato Pie

Servings:6
Cooking Time: 50 Minutes
Ingredients:
- 2 large potatoes
- 4 tablespoons butter, divided
- 1½ teaspoons salt, divided
- 1 teaspoon freshly ground black pepper, divided
- ¾ pound smoked whitefish (such as haddock), cut into bite-size pieces
- ¾ pound skinless salmon fillet, cut into ½-inch pieces
- 1 medium carrot, coarsely grated
- 2 (8-inch) stalks celery, coarsely grated
- 4 cups chopped fresh spinach
- 4 ounces grated sharp white cheddar cheese

Directions:
1. Preheat the oven to 400°F.
2. Bring a pot of salted water to a boil. Add the potatoes and cook for 10 to 12 minutes, until the potatoes are tender. Drain and then mash the potatoes along with 2 tablespoons of the butter, ¾ teaspoon of the salt, and ½ teaspoon of the pepper.
3. In a large baking dish, toss together the smoked fish, salmon, carrot, celery, and spinach. Season with the remaining ¾ teaspoon salt and ½ teaspoon pepper. Spread the mixture out in an even layer. Spread the mashed potatoes over the top in an even layer. Melt the remaining 2 tablespoons of butter and drizzle it over the top. Sprinkle the cheese over the top.
4. Bake in the preheated oven for 30 to 40 minutes, until the top is golden brown and the dish is hot all the way through. Serve immediately.

Nutrition Info:
- InfoCalories: 366; Protein: 34g; Total Fat: 16g; Saturated Fat: 10g; Carbohydrates: 22g; Fiber: 4g; Sodium: 1312mg;

Chimichurri Chicken Drumsticks

Servings:4
Cooking Time: 30 Minutes

Ingredients:

- 8 chicken drumsticks
- 1 cup Chimichurri Sauce, divided

Directions:

1. In a gallon-size zip-top bag, combine the drumsticks with ½ cup chimichurri sauce. Seal the bag and shake to coat. Refrigerate for 8 hours.
2. Preheat the oven to 375°F.
3. Line a rimmed baking sheet with parchment paper.
4. Remove the drumsticks from the bag, pat the marinade off with a paper towel (a little will be left, which is okay), and place them on the prepared baking sheet. Bake for about 30 minutes, or until the juices run clear.
5. Serve with the remaining ½ cup chimichurri sauce on the side.

Nutrition Info:

- InfoCalories:401; Total Fat: 11g; Saturated Fat: 3g; Carbohydrates: 39g; Fiber: 3g; Sodium: 968mg; Protein: 35g

Stuffed Peppers With Ground Turkey

Servings:3
Cooking Time:x

Ingredients:

- 1 tablespoon olive oil
- 1 pound ground turkey
- 1 tablespoon garlic-infused oil, divided
- 1 cup roasted corn kernels
- 2 Roma tomatoes, chopped
- 2 tablespoons pine nuts
- 1 cup cooked brown rice
- 1/2 tablespoon chili powder
- 1/2 teaspoon ground cumin
- 1 teaspoon smoked paprika
- 3 tablespoons chopped fresh cilantro
- 3 large bell peppers: orange, yellow, and green; halved and seeded
- 2 tablespoons coconut oil
- 6 slices goat cheese
- 3 tablespoons Fiesta Salsa (see Chapter 13)

Directions:

1. Preheat oven to 375°F.
2. Heat 1 tablespoon olive oil in a large skillet over medium-high heat and cook ground turkey until browned.
3. Add 1/2 tablespoon garlic-infused oil to skillet along with corn, tomatoes, and pine nuts; stir and heat through.
4. Add brown rice and stir to combine. Stir in remaining 1/2 tablespoon oil, chili powder, cumin, paprika, and cilantro. Remove from heat.
5. Stuff halved peppers with brown rice mixture and brush outside of peppers with coconut oil. Place peppers in an 8" × 8" shallow baking dish.
6. Top each pepper with a slice of goat cheese. Loosely cover dish with foil.
7. Bake 30–40 minutes until peppers are tender. Garnish with salsa.

Nutrition Info:

- InfoCalories: 700,Fat: 43g,Protein: 41g,Sodium: 364mg,Carbohydrates: 41.

Chicken Enchiladas

Servings:8
Cooking Time: 45 Minutes
Ingredients:

- FOR THE SAUCE
- 2 tablespoons grapeseed oil
- 2 tablespoons gluten-free all-purpose flour
- 1 tablespoon Garlic Oil (here)
- ¼ cup gluten-, onion-, and garlic-free chili powder
- ½ teaspoon salt
- ¼ teaspoon ground cumin
- 1 tablespoon minced fresh oregano
- 2 cups homemade (onion- and garlic-free) chicken broth
- FOR THE ENCHILADAS
- Oil for preparing the baking sheet
- 1½ pounds cooked, shredded chicken breast (boneless, skinless)
- 1 cup fresh or frozen (thawed) corn kernels
- 1 (4-ounce) can diced green chiles
- 1 teaspoon ground chipotle
- 1 (14-ounce) can onion- and garlic-free diced tomatoes, drained
- ½ teaspoon salt
- 16 corn tortillas
- 1 cup shredded cheddar or Monterey Jack cheese
- ¼ cup chopped fresh cilantro

Directions:

1. To make the sauce, heat the grapeseed oil in a small saucepan over medium-high heat. Whisk in the flour and cook, stirring, for 1 minute. Stir in the Garlic Oil, chili powder, salt, cumin, and oregano. While stirring constantly, gradually add the broth. Bring to a boil, then reduce the heat to low and simmer, stirring occasionally, for 10 to 15 minutes, until the sauce has thickened. Transfer the sauce to a large, shallow bowl.
2. To make the enchiladas, begin by preheating the oven to 350°F.
3. Oil a 9-by-13-inch baking dish.
4. In a large bowl, combine the chicken, corn, green chiles, ground chipotle, tomatoes, and salt, and stir to mix well. Wrap the tortillas in a clean dish towel, and microwave them on high for about 30 seconds.
5. Coat the bottom of the prepared baking dish with several spoonfuls of the sauce. Dip each tortilla in the sauce to coat it lightly. Spoon about ¼ cup of the chicken mixture into the tortilla in a line down the center. Roll the tortilla up around the filling and place it in the prepared baking dish, seam-side down. Repeat with the remaining tortillas and filling. When all of the tortillas are filled and in the baking dish, spoon the remaining sauce over the top, covering all of the tortillas. Sprinkle with the cheese.
6. Bake the enchiladas in the preheated oven until the sauce is bubbly and the cheese is melted, for 15 to 20 minutes. Serve hot, garnished with cilantro.

Nutrition Info:

- InfoCalories: 415; Protein: 37g; Total Fat: 13g; Saturated Fat: 3g; Carbohydrates: 41g; Fiber: 9g; Sodium: 759mg;

Victor's Chicken Parmesan

Servings:4
Cooking Time:x
Ingredients:

- 3 large eggs
- 3 cups gluten-free panko bread crumbs
- 1⁄16 teaspoon salt
- 1⁄2 teaspoon freshly ground black pepper
- 1 teaspoon dried oregano
- 4 (6-ounce) boneless, skinless chicken breasts, pounded to a 1⁄2" thickness
- 1 tablespoon safflower oil
- 2 cups Basic Marinara Sauce (see Chapter 13)
- 2 cups baby spinach
- 2 cups shredded mozzarella cheese
- 1⁄4 cup grated Parmesan cheese
- 6 whole basil leaves

Directions:

1. Preheat oven to 400°F. Grease a 9" × 13" casserole dish.
2. Whisk eggs in shallow bowl and set aside. Place bread crumbs, salt, pepper, and oregano on a plate. Stir to combine. Dredge chicken in egg, tapping off any excess; dredge in bread crumb mixture and place on a clean plate.
3. Heat oil in a medium skillet over medium-high heat. Add chicken and cook 2–3 minutes per side, or until golden brown.
4. Spoon a thin layer of marinara sauce in casserole dish. Lay down each piece of chicken. Then layer more marinara, and half of the spinach, mozzarella, and 2 tablespoons Parmesan cheese. Repeat again with another layer of the same ingredients.
5. Bake until chicken is cooked through and cheese is melted, about 5–7 minutes. Remove from oven. Garnish with basil.

Nutrition Info:

- InfoCalories: 777,Fat: 28g,Protein: 65g,Sodium: 1,633mg,Carbohydrates: 63.

Turkey Bolognese With Pasta

Servings:4
Cooking Time:x
Ingredients:

* 1 tablespoon olive oil
* 1 large carrot, peeled and diced small
* 1/8 teaspoon wheat-free asafetida powder
* 1 teaspoon salt, divided
* 1/2 teaspoon dried oregano
* 4 ounces pancetta, visible fat discarded and pancetta minced
* 1 pound ground turkey
* 2 tablespoons Tomato Paste (see Chapter 13)
* 1/2 cup Lambrusco wine
* 1 (14-ounce) can San Marzano tomatoes
* 1 tablespoon balsamic vinegar
* 1 pound gluten-free angel hair pasta
* 1/4 cup shaved Parmesan cheese

Directions:

1. Heat oil in a wide, deep skillet or saucepan over medium heat. Add carrots, asafetida, 1/2 teaspoon salt, and oregano and cook for 6 minutes. Add pancetta and continue cooking everything until carrots are softened, 8–10 minutes.
2. Add ground turkey and remaining 1/2 teaspoon salt. Cook until meat is lightly browned. Add tomato paste and cook 2–3 minutes.
3. Add wine. Cook until wine has reduced by half, 4–5 minutes.
4. Add tomatoes and stir. Cook 5 minutes. Stir balsamic vinegar into sauce. Set heat to low and simmer.
5. Meanwhile, cook pasta according to package directions. Drain. Stir Parmesan into pasta and top with Bolognese sauce.

Nutrition Info:

* InfoCalories: 528,Fat: 18g,Protein: 40g,Sodium: 1,010mg,Carbohydrates: 93.

Thai Sweet Chili Broiled Salmon

Servings:4
Cooking Time: 10 Minutes
Ingredients:

* 6 tablespoons homemade Thai Sweet Chili Sauce (here)
* 3 tablespoons gluten-free soy sauce
* 1 tablespoon finely grated fresh ginger
* 4 (6-ounce) salmon fillets
* 2 scallions (green part only), thinly sliced
* 1 tablespoon chopped fresh cilantro
* 1½ teaspoons toasted sesame seeds

Directions:

1. In a large bowl, combine the chili sauce, soy sauce, and ginger, and mix well. Add the fish, turning until evenly coated. Cover the bowl and marinate fish in the refrigerator for 30 minutes.
2. To cook the fish, heat the broiler to high and line a rimmed baking sheet with foil.
3. Arrange the salmon fillets skin-side down on the prepared baking sheet. Brush some of the marinade over the fish, coating generously. Broil for about 8 to 10 minutes, until just cooked through. Serve immediately, garnished with scallions, cilantro, and sesame seeds.

Nutrition Info:

* InfoCalories: 291; Protein: 34g; Total Fat: 11g; Saturated Fat: 2g; Carbohydrates: 13g; Fiber: 1g; Sodium: 812mg;

Roasted Garlic Shrimp And Red Peppers

Servings:4
Cooking Time: 17 Minutes
Ingredients:

- 2 pounds peeled and deveined shrimp (tails left intact)
- 2 red bell peppers, cut into 1½-inch triangles
- 4 tablespoons Garlic Oil (here)
- 1½ tablespoons smoked paprika
- ¾ teaspoon cayenne
- 1 teaspoon salt
- ½ teaspoon freshly ground black pepper
- 1 tablespoon chopped fresh oregano

Directions:

1. Preheat the oven to 400°F.
2. In a large baking dish, combine the shrimp, peppers, Garlic Oil, paprika, cayenne, salt, and pepper, and toss to coat. Spread the shrimp and peppers out in a single layer.
3. Roast the shrimp and peppers in the preheated oven for 10 minutes. Using tongs, flip the shrimp and peppers over, sprinkle the oregano over the top, and continue to roast for another 5 to 7 minutes, until the shrimp are cooked through. Serve hot.

Nutrition Info:

- InfoCalories: 260; Protein: 50g; Total Fat: 4g; Saturated Fat: 0g; Carbohydrates: 9g; Fiber: 3g; Sodium: 1099mg;

Red Snapper With Creole Sauce

Servings:4
Cooking Time: 20 Minutes
Ingredients:

- 1 tablespoon olive oil
- 1 tablespoon Garlic Oil (here)
- ½ medium green bell pepper, diced
- 1 (14½-ounce) can onion- and garlic-free diced tomatoes with juice
- 2 scallions (green part only), thinly sliced
- 1 tablespoon red-wine vinegar
- 1 teaspoon gluten-free soy sauce or coconut aminos
- ½ teaspoon dried basil
- ½ teaspoon salt
- ½ teaspoon freshly ground black pepper
- Dash of hot-pepper sauce
- 4 (6-ounce) red-snapper fillets
- ¼ cup chopped fresh basil

Directions:

1. Heat the olive oil and Garlic Oil in a large skillet over medium-high heat. Add the bell pepper and cook, stirring, until softened, for about 5 minutes. Add the tomatoes with their juice, scallions, vinegar, soy sauce, basil, salt, pepper, and hot sauce and bring to a boil.
2. Reduce the heat to low, add the fish, and spoon the saucy tomato mixture over the top. Cover the pan and cook until the fish is cooked through and flakes easily with a fork, for about 10 minutes. Serve immediately, with sauce spooned over the top and garnished with basil.

Nutrition Info:

- InfoCalories: 281; Protein: 46g; Total Fat: 7g; Saturated Fat: 1g; Carbohydrates: 7g; Fiber: 2g; Sodium: 588mg;

Soy-infused Roast Chicken

Servings:4
Cooking Time:x
Ingredients:

- ½ cup (125 ml) gluten-free soy sauce
- 2 tablespoons plus 2 teaspoons sesame oil
- 2 heaping tablespoons light brown sugar
- 2 teaspoons grated ginger
- 3 star anise (or 2 teaspoons ground star anise)
- ½ teaspoon ground cinnamon
- One 4-pound (1.8 kg) whole chicken, excess fat removed
- 2 cups (500 ml) gluten-free, onion-free chicken stock*
- Vegetables, for serving

Directions:

1. Combine the soy sauce, sesame oil, brown sugar, ginger, star anise, and cinnamon in a bowl and stir until the sugar has dissolved. Place the chicken, breast up, in a baking dish. Pour the marinade over it and use a pastry brush to ensure the entire chicken is well coated. Cover and refrigerate for 3 to 4 hours, brushing the chicken with the marinade every 1 to 2 hours.
2. Preheat the oven to 350°F (180°C).
3. Uncover the chicken, pour the stock into the baking dish, and roast for 30 minutes. Cover loosely with foil and roast for 20 to 30 minutes more, until the juices run clear when you piece the chicken with a toothpick in the thickest part of the thigh. Let rest for a few minutes before carving.
4. Serve with the pan juices and your choice of vegetables.

Nutrition Info:

- Info304 calories; 40 g protein; 12 g total fat; 2 g saturated fat; 6 g carbohydrates; 0 g fiber; 1485 mg sodium

Pan-seared Scallops With Sautéed Kale

Servings:4
Cooking Time: 15 Minutes
Ingredients:

- 2 tablespoons extra-virgin olive oil
- 1 pound sea scallops
- ½ teaspoon sea salt
- ⅛ teaspoon freshly ground black pepper
- 3 cups stemmed, chopped kale leaves
- Juice of 1 orange
- Zest of 1 orange

Directions:

1. In a large nonstick skillet over medium-high heat, heat the olive oil until it shimmers. Swirl the pan to coat it with the oil.
2. Season the scallops with salt and pepper. Add them to the hot skillet and cook for about 3 minutes per side. Transfer the scallops to a platter and tent with foil to keep warm. Return the skillet to the heat.
3. Add the kale to the skillet. Cook for about 5 minutes, stirring.
4. Add the orange juice and zest. Cook for 3 minutes more.
5. Serve the scallops on top of the sautéed kale.

Nutrition Info:

- InfoCalories:199; Total Fat: 8g; Saturated Fat: 1g; Carbohydrates: 11g; Fiber: <1g; Sodium: 439mg; Protein: 21g

Orange Chicken And Broccoli Stir-fry

Servings:4
Cooking Time:x
Ingredients:

- 2 tablespoons fresh orange juice
- 2 tablespoons fresh lemon juice
- 2 tablespoons gluten-free soy sauce (tamari)
- 2 tablespoons orange marmalade (without high-fructose corn syrup)
- 2 teaspoons cornstarch
- 2 tablespoons safflower oil
- 2 pounds chicken tenders, cut into 1" pieces
- 1 1/2 pounds broccoli, cut into florets
- 1 medium red bell pepper, seeded and chopped
- 1 green onion, chopped, green part only
- 2 teaspoons chopped fresh gingerroot
- 1 teaspoon chili powder

Directions:

1. In a small bowl, combine orange juice, lemon juice, soy sauce, marmalade, and cornstarch. Set aside.
2. Heat oil over medium-high heat in a wok or 9" nonstick skillet. Add chicken and stir until cooked through, 2–3 minutes. Transfer chicken to a plate.
3. Add broccoli to wok and cook 3 minutes. Increase heat to high, add bell pepper and cook 2 minutes, stirring frequently. Transfer vegetables to plate with chicken.
4. Reduce heat to medium-high and add onion, ginger, and chili powder. Cook until fragrant, about 30 seconds.
5. Add orange sauce to pan and cook until slightly thickened, about 30 seconds. Add chicken and vegetables to wok and toss to coat.

Nutrition Info:

- InfoCalories: 424,Fat: 13g,Protein: 53g,Sodium: 780mg,Carbohydrates: 23.

Cumin Turkey With Fennel

Servings:4
Cooking Time:x
Ingredients:

- 1 tablespoon brown sugar
- 1/4 teaspoon ground cinnamon
- 1/2 tablespoon ground cumin
- 1/4 teaspoon kosher salt
- 1/2 teaspoon freshly ground black pepper
- 1/4 teaspoon cayenne pepper
- 1 cup cubed celeriac
- 1 cup halved seedless red grapes
- 1 fennel bulb (about 1/2 pound), cut into 1" chunks
- 1 tablespoon olive oil
- 2 pounds lean turkey fillets

Directions:

1. Preheat oven to 425°F. Position rack in upper third of oven.
2. Mix brown sugar, cinnamon, cumin, salt, pepper, and cayenne in a small bowl.
3. In a medium bowl, combine celeriac, grapes, and fennel with oil and half of spice mixture. Spread out evenly in a single layer in an 18" × 13" rimmed baking sheet.
4. Rub remaining spice mixture on both sides of turkey fillets and place on top of grapes and vegetables.
5. Bake 40 minutes; check at 30 minutes to be sure food is not burning—if so, move pan to a lower rack.

Nutrition Info:

- InfoCalories: 354,Fat: 7g,Protein: 52g,Sodium: 357mg,Carbohydrates: 19.

Sweet And Savory Brazilian Meat And Cheese Tart

Servings:6
Cooking Time:x

Ingredients:

- 2 1/2 cups gluten-free all-purpose flour
- 1/2 cup butter
- 1/2 cup vegetable shortening
- 1 teaspoon salt, divided
- 1 teaspoon turbinado sugar
- 4–6 tablespoons ice water, for blending
- 1 tablespoon coconut oil, divided
- 2 pounds ground beef
- 1/8 teaspoon wheat-free asafetida powder
- 2 bunches spinach, finely chopped (stems removed)
- 1/2 teaspoon freshly ground black pepper
- 1/4 teaspoon cayenne pepper
- 1/2 cup grated Parmesan cheese
- 6 large eggs
- 1 egg beaten with 1 tablespoon water (egg wash)
- 4 medium limes, cut in quarters

Directions:

1. For the pie crust: In a bowl of a stand mixer fitted with a paddle attachment (or using a pastry cutter or two knives), combine flour, butter, vegetable shortening, 1/2 teaspoon salt, and sugar; work dough until mixture resembles oatmeal. Slowly add ice water and mix until pliable but not very wet. Wrap in plastic wrap and refrigerate 30 minutes. Dough can be kept in refrigerator up to 3 days or frozen up to 3 months.
2. Preheat oven to 375°F.
3. For the filling: In a medium saucepan on medium-high heat, warm half of coconut oil and add ground beef, breaking up into pieces and cooking until browned. Add remaining oil, asafetida, spinach, remaining salt, pepper, and cayenne pepper. Cook 2–3 minutes or until spinach is wilted. Remove from heat and mix in Parmesan. If there is any extra juice, drain first before putting filling into pie.
4. Take half of dough out of refrigerator. Cover your work surface with flour and sprinkle more flour onto rolling pin and dough. Working quickly, roll dough until it's about 18", a little larger than size of 9" pie dish. Dust dough with flour occasionally to ensure it does not stick to surface or rolling pin. Transfer dough to pie dish. Gently tuck dough inside dish and allow remaining dough to drape over sides of dish. Prick pie crust all over with a fork.
5. Pour filling into 9" pie dish and spread out evenly. Make 6 small holes in filling, evenly around dish, and slowly drop 1 egg into each hole. Roll out remaining dough with flour and drape it on top of filling and eggs. Using your fingers, seal crust around edges. Cut 2–3 slits on top to vent during baking.
6. Brush egg wash all over top and place into middle rack of oven. Bake 50–55 minutes or until crust is golden brown. Let cool 15 minutes before slicing and serving with lime wedges.

Nutrition Info:

- InfoCalories: 927,Fat: 59g,Protein: 50g,Sodium: 795mg,Carbohydrates: 51.

Lemon-pepper Shrimp

Servings:4
Cooking Time: 8 Minutes

Ingredients:

- 2 tablespoons Garlic Oil
- 1 pound medium shrimp, shelled and deveined
- Juice of 2 lemons
- 1/2 teaspoon sea salt
- 1/2 teaspoon freshly ground black pepper

Directions:

1. In a large nonstick skillet over medium-high heat, heat the garlic oil until it shimmers.
2. Add the shrimp. Cook for about 5 minutes, stirring occasionally, until it is pink.
3. Squeeze in the lemon juice, then add the salt and pepper. Simmer for 3 minutes more.

Nutrition Info:

- InfoCalories:119; Total Fat: 2g; Saturated Fat: 0g; Carbohydrates: 2g; Fiber: 0g; Sodium: 494mg; Protein: 25g

Tarragon Chicken Terrine

Servings:8
Cooking Time:x
Ingredients:

- 2 teaspoons garlic-infused olive oil
- 2 tablespoons olive oil
- 2 tablespoons (30 g) salted butter
- ¼ cup (60 ml) dry white wine
- 14 ounces (400 g) boneless, skinless chicken thighs, excess fat removed, finely chopped
- 12 ounces (340 g) ground white meat chicken
- Nine 1-ounce (28 g) slices gluten-free, soy-free bread, crusts removed, crumbled into coarse crumbs
- 1 large egg, lightly beaten
- ½ cup (125 ml) light cream
- Small handful of flat-leaf parsley leaves, chopped
- Small handful of tarragon leaves, chopped
- Salt and freshly ground black pepper
- 14 long, thin prosciutto slices (about 12 ounces/340 g total)
- Boiling water
- Green salad, for serving

Directions:

1. Preheat the oven to 350°F (180°C).
2. Heat the garlic-infused oil, olive oil, and butter in a small heavy-bottomed frying pan over medium heat until the butter has melted. Stir in the wine and set aside.
3. Place the chicken thigh meat, ground chicken, bread crumbs, egg, cream, parsley, and tarragon in a large bowl, pour in the wine mixture, and mix together well. Season with the salt and pepper.
4. Line a deep 8 x 4-inch (20 x 10 cm) loaf pan with overlapping slices of prosciutto, leaving a little overhang on both long sides. Spoon the chicken mixture into the pan and smooth the surface. Fold in the overhanging prosciutto to enclose the filling. Cover the pan with foil and place in a large baking dish. Pour enough boiling water into the dish to come two thirds of the way up the side of the pan.
5. Bake for 1 hour, or until the juices run clear when a toothpick is inserted into the center of the terrine. Set aside to cool to room temperature.
6. Remove the foil and invert the pan onto a wire rack over the baking dish to allow the juices to drain away. After the juices stop running, turn the pan upright and cover again with foil. Top with another loaf pan containing two or three heavy cans, to compress the terrine. Place in the refrigerator for a few hours or overnight.
7. To serve, remove the weights, extra pan, and foil, turn out the terrine onto a cutting board, and pat dry with paper towel. Cut into thick slices and serve with your favorite salad.

Nutrition Info:

- Info439 calories; 32 g protein; 27 g total fat; 5 g saturated fat; 15 g carbohydrates; 1 g fiber; 922 mg sodium

Orange-ginger Salmon

Servings:4
Cooking Time: 12 Minutes
Ingredients:

- ¼ cup Garlic Oil
- Juice of 2 oranges
- 2 tablespoons gluten-free soy sauce
- 1 tablespoon peeled and grated fresh ginger
- 1 pound salmon fillet, quartered

Directions:

1. Preheat the oven to 450°F.
2. In a shallow baking dish, whisk together the garlic oil, orange juice, soy sauce, and ginger.
3. Place the salmon, flesh-side down, in the marinade. Marinate for 10 minutes.
4. Place the salmon, skin-side up, on a rimmed baking sheet. Bake for 12 to 15 minutes, until opaque.

Nutrition Info:

- InfoCalories:282; Total Fat: 20g; Saturated Fat: 3g; Carbohydrates: 5g; Fiber: 0g; Sodium: 553mg; Protein: 23g

Barbecue Chicken

Servings:4

Cooking Time: 30 Minutes

Ingredients:

- 8 chicken drumsticks
- 1 recipe Homemade Barbecue Sauce

Directions:

1. Preheat the oven to 375°F.
2. Place the chicken pieces in a large baking dish and brush them on all sides with the barbecue sauce.
3. Bake for about 30 minutes, or until the juices run clear.

Nutrition Info:

- InfoCalories:155; Total Fat: 6g; Saturated Fat: 1g; Carbohydrates: 5g; Fiber: 1g; Sodium: 328mg; Protein: 26g

Pork And Vegetable Fricassee With Buttered Quinoa

Servings:6

Cooking Time:x

Ingredients:

- ¼ cup (35 g) cornstarch
- Salt and freshly ground black pepper
- 2 pounds (900 g) lean pork, diced
- 2 teaspoons garlic-infused olive oil
- 2 teaspoons olive oil
- One 14.5-ounce (400 g) can crushed tomatoes
- ½ cup (125 ml) tomato puree
- 2 carrots, sliced
- 1½ cups (375 ml) gluten-free, onion-free beef or vegetable stock*
- 1 large rosemary sprig
- 4 ounces (120 g) baby spinach leaves (4 cups)
- 7 ounces (200 g) green beans, trimmed and halved (2 cups)
- ⅔ cup (70 g) quinoa
- 1 tablespoon (15 g) salted butter
- Salt and freshly ground black pepper

Directions:

1. Place the cornstarch, salt, and pepper in a shallow bowl. Dust the pork in the cornstarch, shaking off any excess.
2. Heat the garlic-infused oil and olive oil in a large heavy-bottomed saucepan or stockpot over medium-high heat. Add one third of the pork and cook, stirring, for 2 to 3 minutes, until golden. Transfer to a plate with a slotted spoon and cover to keep warm. Repeat with the remaining pork.
3. Add the tomatoes, tomato puree, carrots, stock, and rosemary to the final batch of pork, then return the reserved pork and any juices to the pot. Bring to a boil, then reduce the heat to a simmer. Cover and cook, stirring occasionally, for 1 hour, or until the pork is very tender.
4. Remove the pan from the heat and remove the rosemary stem (the leaves should have cooked off). Stir in the spinach and green beans, then season to taste with salt and pepper. Cook for 5 minutes, or until the beans have softened.
5. Meanwhile, bring a medium saucepan of water to a boil. Add the quinoa and boil for 10 to 12 minutes, until just tender. Drain and rinse under hot water, then drain again. Stir in the butter until melted and season to taste with salt and pepper.
6. Divide the quinoa among shallow bowls and serve with a generous helping of the fricassee.

Nutrition Info:

- Info409 calories; 36 g protein; 14 g total fat; 5 g saturated fat; 31 g carbohydrates; 6 g fiber; 611 mg sodium

Beef Stir-fry With Chinese Broccoli And Green Beans

Servings:4
Cooking Time:x
Ingredients:

- 1 heaping tablespoon grated ginger
- 2 teaspoons garlic-infused olive oil
- 2 teaspoons olive oil
- ¼ cup (60 ml) sesame oil
- 1 pound (450 g) beef sirloin or top round steak, very thinly sliced
- 1 bunch Chinese broccoli, cut into 1-inch (3 cm) lengths
- 7 ounces (200 g) green beans, trimmed (1¾ cups)
- 1 cup (80 g) bean sprouts
- 1 tablespoon gluten-free, onion-free, garlic-free oyster sauce
- ¼ teaspoon cayenne pepper
- Steamed rice or prepared rice noodles, for serving

Directions:

1. Combine the ginger, garlic-infused oil, olive oil, and 2 tablespoons of the sesame oil in a bowl. Add the beef and toss to coat. Cover and refrigerate for 2 to 3 hours.
2. Heat the remaining 2 tablespoons of sesame oil in a wok over medium-high heat. Add the beef and cook for 2 minutes, or until lightly browned. Add the Chinese broccoli, green beans, and bean sprouts and stir-fry for 2 to 4 minutes, until the ingredients are tender. Pour in the oyster sauce and cayenne pepper and stir-fry for 1 to 2 minutes, until the sauce is warmed through and the beef and vegetables are coated.
3. Serve over rice or rice noodles.

Nutrition Info:

- Info437 calories; 24 g protein; 34 g total fat; 6 g saturated fat; 7 g carbohydrates; 3 g fiber; 92 mg sodium

Spanish Meatloaf With Garlic Mashed Potatoes

Servings:6
Cooking Time:x
Ingredients:

- Nonstick cooking spray
- 1½ pounds (700 g) extra-lean ground beef
- ½ cup (125 ml) tomato paste
- ¾ cup (90 g) dried gluten-free, soy-free bread crumbs*
- 2 large eggs, lightly beaten
- 2 teaspoons garlic-infused olive oil
- 2 teaspoons olive oil
- Small handful of flat-leaf parsley leaves, roughly chopped
- ¾ teaspoon ground ginger
- 1 teaspoon chili powder
- 1½ teaspoons cayenne pepper
- 1½ teaspoons sweet paprika
- Salt and freshly ground black pepper
- 4 potatoes, peeled (if desired) and quartered
- 1 tablespoon garlic-infused olive oil
- 2 tablespoons (30 g) salted butter
- ⅓ cup (80 ml) low-fat milk, lactose-free milk, or suitable plant-based milk
- Salt and freshly ground black pepper
- Green salad or vegetables, for serving

Directions:

1. Preheat the oven to 350°F (180°C). Line an 8½ x 4½-inch (25 x 11.5 cm) loaf pan with foil and spray with cooking spray.
2. Combine the beef, tomato paste, bread crumbs, eggs, garlic-infused oil, olive oil, parsley, ginger, chili powder, cayenne, paprika, salt, and pepper in a large bowl. Mix well with your hands. Press into the loaf pan.
3. Bake for 40 to 45 minutes, until cooked through. (The juices will run clear when you pierce the center with a small knife.) Let rest for at least 5 minutes before serving.
4. Meanwhile, to make the garlic mashed potatoes, cook the potatoes in a saucepan of boiling water until very tender, about 10 minutes. Drain. Mash with a potato masher. Stir in the garlic-infused oil, butter, and milk and season with salt and pepper. Adjust the ingredients for taste or texture if needed.
5. Cut the meatloaf into thick slices and serve with a generous spoonful (or two) of mashed potatoes and your choice of salad or vegetables.

Nutrition Info:

- Info437 calories; 29 g protein; 23 g total fat; 8 g saturated fat; 28 g carbohydrates; 3 g fiber; 370 mg sodium

Coq Au Vin

Servings:4
Cooking Time:x
Ingredients:

- 1 (2-pound) whole free-range chicken, cut into 8 serving pieces
- 1⁄4 teaspoon salt
- 1⁄2 teaspoon freshly ground black pepper
- 2 tablespoons gluten-free all-purpose flour
- 1 tablespoon garlic-infused olive oil
- 1⁄4 cup butter
- 1⁄4 pound bacon (preferably smoked), cut into short strips
- 1 large carrot, peeled and diced
- 1 medium stalk celery, diced
- 3 cups Beaujolais wine
- 13⁄4 cups Easy Onion- and Garlic-Free Chicken Stock (see Chapter 4)
- 2 bay leaves
- 1 cup finely chopped fresh flat-leaf parsley

Directions:

1. Place chicken pieces in a large bowl and toss with salt, pepper, and flour until well coated.
2. Heat oil and butter in a large, wide ovenproof pan over medium heat and brown chicken on all sides; work in batches if necessary to avoid overcrowding the pan. Remove and set aside.
3. Add bacon to pan and cook until lightly browned, 3–4 minutes. Remove with a slotted spoon and set aside with chicken. Add carrot and celery and cook 5 minutes or until softened and lightly browned. Set aside.
4. Add wine to pan and stir well; add stock and bay leaves, and return vegetables, chicken, and bacon to pan. Heat until just about boiling, reduce heat to low, and simmer uncovered for 30 minutes or until chicken is cooked through.
5. Remove chicken pieces, increase heat, and simmer sauce until reduced, thickened, and glossy, about 25 minutes.
6. Return chicken to pan and serve immediately. Garnish with parsley.

Nutrition Info:

- InfoCalories: 592,Fat: 29g,Protein: 44g,Sodium: 594mg,Carbohydrates: 12.

Chicken And Rice With Peanut Sauce

Servings:4
Cooking Time: 10 Minutes
Ingredients:

- 2 tablespoons Garlic Oil
- 1 pound boneless skinless chicken thigh meat, cut into strips
- ½ cup sugar-free natural peanut butter
- ½ cup coconut milk
- 2 tablespoons gluten-free soy sauce
- 1 tablespoon peeled and grated fresh ginger
- Juice of 1 lime
- 2 cups cooked brown rice

Directions:

1. In a large nonstick skillet over medium-high heat, heat the garlic oil until it shimmers.
2. Add the chicken and cook for about 6 minutes, stirring occasionally, until browned.
3. In a small bowl, whisk the peanut butter, coconut milk, soy sauce, ginger, and lime juice. Add this to the chicken.
4. Mix in the rice. Cook for 3 minutes more, stirring.

Nutrition Info:

- InfoCalories:718; Total Fat: 40g; Saturated Fat: 13g; Carbohydrates: 46g; Fiber: 5g; Sodium: 757mg; Protein: 46g

Tuna And Pineapple Burgers

Servings:4
Cooking Time: 10 Minutes

Ingredients:

- 1 pound canned tuna, flaked
- ½ cup gluten-free bread crumbs
- 1 egg, beaten
- ¼ cup plus 2 tablespoons Low-FODMAP Mayonnaise, divided
- Zest of 1 lemon
- ½ teaspoon sea salt
- ⅛ teaspoon freshly ground black pepper
- 2 tablespoons Garlic Oil
- 3 tablespoons Teriyaki Sauce
- 4 canned pineapple slices, packed in water, drained
- 4 gluten-free hamburger buns

Directions:

1. In a large bowl, mix the tuna, bread crumbs, egg, 2 tablespoons mayonnaise, lemon zest, salt, and pepper until thoroughly combined. Form the tuna mixture into 4 patties.

2. In a large nonstick skillet over medium-high heat, heat the garlic oil until it shimmers.

3. Add the patties and cook for 5 minutes per side.

4. While the burgers cook, in a small bowl, whisk together the teriyaki sauce and remaining ¼ cup mayonnaise. Spread the sauce on the buns.

5. Place 1 cooked burger in each bun and top with 1 pineapple slice.

Nutrition Info:

- InfoCalories:495; Total Fat: 18g; Saturated Fat: 4g; Carbohydrates: 42g; Fiber: 2g; Sodium: 1,270mg; Protein: 39g

Vegetarian And Vegan Recipes

Zucchini Pasta Alla Puttanesca

Servings:4
Cooking Time: 15 Minutes
Ingredients:
- 2 tablespoons olive oil
- 1½ cups diced tomatoes
- 1 tablespoon Garlic Oil (here)
- 2 tablespoons chopped Kalamata olives
- 1 tablespoon capers, drained
- 1 teaspoon salt
- ½ teaspoon freshly ground black pepper
- ½ teaspoon red pepper flakes
- ¼ cup chopped fresh basil
- 3 large zucchini, cut into ribbons with a spiral slicer
- ½ cup freshly grated Parmesan cheese

Directions:
1. Heat the olive oil in a large skillet over medium-high heat. Add the tomatoes and Garlic Oil, and cook for about 10 minutes, until the tomatoes begin to break down and become saucy. Add the olives, capers, salt, pepper, and red pepper flakes, and cook for 5 minutes more. Stir in the basil.
2. Remove the pan from the heat and add the zucchini. Toss until the zucchini noodles soften and are well coated with the sauce. Serve immediately, garnished with Parmesan cheese.

Nutrition Info:
- InfoCalories: 226; Protein: 14g; Total Fat: 15g; Saturated Fat: 5g; Carbohydrates: 16g; Fiber: 5g; Sodium: 974mg;

Chipotle Tofu And Sweet Potato Tacos With Avocado Salsa

Servings:4
Cooking Time: 20 Minutes
Ingredients:
- FOR THE FILLING
- 2 tablespoons olive oil
- 2 sweet potatoes, peeled and cut into ½-inch cubes
- 1 pound firm tofu, diced
- ½ to 1 teaspoon ground chipotle chiles
- 2 tablespoons sugar
- Juice of 1 lime
- FOR THE AVOCADO SALSA
- 2 tomatoes
- ½ avocado, diced
- ¼ serrano chile, diced
- Juice of ½ lime
- ¼ teaspoon salt
- 2 tablespoons chopped fresh cilantro
- TO SERVE
- 8 soft corn tortillas

Directions:
1. Heat the olive oil in a large skillet over medium heat. Add the sweet potatoes and cook for about 5 minutes, until the potatoes begin to soften. Add the tofu, chipotle, sugar, and lime juice. Reduce the heat to low and cook, stirring occasionally, until the sweet potatoes are tender, about 15 minutes.
2. Meanwhile, wrap the tortillas in aluminum foil and heat them in a 350°F oven for 10 minutes.
3. To make the avocado salsa, combine the tomatoes, avocado, chile, lime juice, and salt in a medium bowl. Stir in the cilantro.
4. To serve, fill the tortillas with the filliing, dividing equally, and spoon a dollop of avocado salsa on top of each. Serve immediately.

Nutrition Info:
- InfoCalories: 421; Protein: 15g; Total Fat: 18g; Saturated Fat: 3g; Carbohydrates: 55g; Fiber: 10g; Sodium: 229mg;

Quinoa-stuffed Eggplant Roulades With Feta And Mint

Servings:4

Cooking Time: 45 Minutes

Ingredients:

- 3 tablespoons olive oil, divided
- ½ cup uncooked quinoa, rinsed
- 1 cup water
- ¼ cup toasted pine nuts
- 2 medium eggplants, sliced lengthwise into ¼-inch-thick slices
- ½ teaspoon salt
- ½ teaspoon freshly ground black pepper
- 1½ cups onion- and garlic-free tomato sauce or marinara sauce (such as Rao's Sensitive Formula Marinara Sauce)
- 2 tablespoons chopped fresh mint
- ½ cup crumbled feta cheese

Directions:

1. Preheat the oven to 375°F.
2. Grease a large baking dish with 1 tablespoon of the olive oil.
3. In a small saucepan, combine the quinoa and water, and bring to a boil over high heat. Reduce the heat to low, cover, and simmer for about 15 minutes, until the water has evaporated and the quinoa is tender. Stir in the pine nuts.
4. While the quinoa is cooking, prepare the eggplant slices. Heat the remaining 2 tablespoons of olive oil in a large skillet over medium-high heat. Sprinkle the eggplant slices on both sides with salt and pepper, and add them to the pan, cooking in a single layer (you'll need to cook them in batches). Cook for about 3 minutes per side, until golden brown. Transfer the eggplant slices to a plate as they are cooked.
5. To make the roulades, lay an eggplant slice on your work surface and spoon some of the quinoa onto the bottom. Roll the eggplant up into a tube around the filling. Place the rolls as you complete them into a baking dish, and spoon the marinara sauce over the top. Sprinkle the mint and cheese over the roulades, and bake in the preheated oven until they are heated through and the sauce is bubbly, for about 15 minutes.

Nutrition Info:

- InfoCalories: 422; Protein: 11g; Total Fat: 25g; Saturated Fat: 6g; Carbohydrates: 44g; Fiber: 14g; Sodium: 894mg;

Watercress Zucchini Soup

Servings:4

Cooking Time: 15 Minutes

Ingredients:

- 2 tablespoons extra-virgin olive oil
- 1 leek, white part removed and the greens finely chopped
- 3 cups homemade (onion- and garlic-free) vegetable broth
- 1 pound zucchini, chopped
- 8 ounces chopped watercress
- 2 tablespoons dried tarragon
- 1 teaspoon salt
- ¼ teaspoon freshly ground black pepper
- 2 tablespoons heavy cream

Directions:

1. In a large pot, heat the olive oil over medium-high heat until it shimmers.
2. Add the leek greens and cook, stirring occasionally, until the vegetables are soft, about seven minutes.
3. Add the vegetable broth and zucchini and simmer, stirring occasionally, for eight minutes.
4. Add the watercress, tarragon, salt, and pepper. Cook, stirring occasionally, an additional five minutes.
5. Carefully transfer the soup mixture to a blender or food processor. You may need to work in batches.
6. Fold a towel and place it over the top of the blender with your hand on top of it. Purée the soup for 30 seconds, and then remove the lid to vent steam. Close the blender and purée for another 30 seconds, until the mixture is smooth.
7. Transfer the mixture back to the cooking pot and stir in the heavy cream. Serve immediately.

Nutrition Info:

- InfoCalories: 161; Total Fat: 11g; Saturated Fat: 3g; Cholesterol: 10mg; Carbohydrates: 9g; Fiber: 2g; Protein: 7g;

Pasta With Pesto Sauce

Servings:4
Cooking Time: 0 Minutes
Ingredients:
- 8 ounces gluten-free angel hair pasta, cooked according to the package instructions. Drained
- 1 recipe Macadamia Spinach Pesto
- ¼ cup grated Parmesan cheese

Directions:
1. In the warm pot that you used to cook the pasta, toss the noodles with the pesto.
2. Sprinkle with the cheese.

Nutrition Info:
- InfoCalories:449; Total Fat: 25g; Saturated Fat: 6g; Carbohydrates: 46g; Fiber: 3g; Sodium: 444mg; Protein: 13g

Baked Tofu Báhn Mì Lettuce Wrap

Servings:4
Cooking Time: 20 Minutes
Ingredients:
- FOR THE TOFU
- 1 (16-ounce) package firm tofu, drained and cut into ½-inch-thick slabs
- 2 tablespoons gluten-free soy sauce
- 2 teaspoons grated fresh ginger
- Vegetable oil or coconut oil to prepare the baking sheet
- FOR THE VEGETABLES
- ½ cup rice vinegar
- ¼ cup water
- ¼ cup sugar
- 1 teaspoon salt
- 1½ cups shredded carrot
- 1½ cups shredded daikon radish
- FOR THE WRAPS
- 8 large lettuce leaves
- 2 tablespoons mayonnaise
- ½ medium cucumber, peeled, seeded, and cut into matchsticks
- 2 large jalapeño chiles, thinly sliced
- 1 cup cilantro leaves

Directions:
1. Line a rimmed baking sheet with paper towels and place the cut tofu on the sheet in a single layer. Top with another layer of paper towels and then another baking sheet. Weight the top baking sheet down with something heavy (cans of tomatoes or beans work well). Let sit for 30 minutes.
2. While the tofu is draining, prepare the vegetables. In a small saucepan, combine the vinegar, water, sugar, and salt and cook, stirring, over medium heat, until the sugar has dissolved, for about 3 minutes. Remove the pan from the heat and add the carrot and daikon, stirring to coat well. Let sit for 20 minutes.
3. In a large bowl, combine the soy sauce and ginger. Add the pressed tofu and toss to coat well.
4. Let the tofu sit for about 15 minutes, and preheat the oven to 350°F.
5. Oil a large baking sheet with vegetable or coconut oil.
6. Arrange the tofu slabs in a single layer on the prepared baking sheet and bake in the preheated oven for about 10 minutes. Turn the pieces over and bake for another 10 minutes, until the tofu is browned. Remove from the oven and cut into 1-inch-wide sticks.
7. To make the wraps, arrange the lettuce leaves on your work surface and spread a bit of mayonnaise on each, dividing equally. Fill with the baked tofu, cucumber, chiles, and cilantro. Drain the pickled carrots and daikon, and place a handful onto each wrap. Serve immediately.

Nutrition Info:
- InfoCalories: 180; Protein: 6g; Total Fat: 3g; Saturated Fat: 0g; Carbohydrates: 28g; Fiber: 2g; Sodium: 4138mg;

Spanish Rice

Servings:4
Cooking Time: 10 Minutes
Ingredients:

- 2 tablespoons Garlic Oil
- 6 scallions, green parts only, chopped
- 2 cups hot cooked brown rice
- 1 cup canned crushed tomatoes, drained
- ½ cup Low-FODMAP Vegetable Broth
- ½ cup chopped black olives
- ½ cup pine nuts
- 1 teaspoon dried oregano
- ½ teaspoon sea salt
- ¼ teaspoon freshly ground black pepper

Directions:

1. In a large skillet over medium-high heat, heat the garlic oil until it shimmers.
2. Add the scallions. Cook for 3 minutes, stirring occasionally.
3. Stir in the brown rice, tomatoes, broth, olives, pine nuts, oregano, salt, and pepper. Cook for about 5 minutes more, stirring, until warmed through.

Nutrition Info:

- InfoCalories:399; Total Fat: 22g; Saturated Fat: 2g; Carbohydrates: 46g; Fiber: 6g; Sodium: 506mg; Protein: 8g

Stuffed Zucchini Boats

Servings:4
Cooking Time: 40 Minutes
Ingredients:

- 4 medium zucchini, halved lengthwise with the middles scooped out, chopped, and reserved
- 2 cups cooked brown rice
- ½ cup canned crushed tomatoes, drained
- ½ cup grated Parmesan cheese
- ¼ cup chopped fresh basil leaves
- ½ teaspoon sea salt
- ⅛ teaspoon freshly ground black pepper

Directions:

1. Preheat the oven to 400°F.
2. Place the zucchini halves on a rimmed baking sheet, cut-side up.
3. In a medium bowl, stir together the brown rice, reserved chopped zucchini, tomatoes, Parmesan cheese, basil, salt, and pepper. Spoon the mixture into the zucchini boats.
4. Bake for 40 to 45 minutes, until the zucchini are soft.

Nutrition Info:

- InfoCalories:262; Total Fat: 5g; Saturated Fat: 2g; Carbohydrates: 46g; Fiber: 5g; Sodium: 447mg; Protein: 11g

Savory Baked Tofu

Servings:4
Cooking Time:x
Ingredients:

- 1 (14-ounce) package firm tofu, drained and patted dry
- 2 teaspoons paprika
- 1/16 teaspoon wheat-free asafetida powder
- 2 teaspoons curry powder
- 2 tablespoons extra-virgin olive oil

Directions:

1. Preheat oven to 400°F.
2. Cut tofu widthwise into 1/2" slices.
3. Lay tofu in a lightly greased 9" × 13" casserole dish. Sprinkle on paprika, asafetida, and curry powder, and drizzle with olive oil. Bake 30 minutes.

Nutrition Info:

- InfoCalories: 677,Fat: 33g,Protein: 68g,Sodium: 355mg,Carbohydrates: 26.

Smoky Corn Chowder With Red Peppers

Servings:4
Cooking Time: 45 Minutes
Ingredients:

- 1 tablespoon olive oil
- 1 tablespoon Garlic Oil (here)
- 1 (10-inch) stalk celery, diced
- 2 carrots, diced
- 1 leek (green part only), halved lengthwise and thinly sliced
- 2 red bell peppers, seeded and diced
- 4 Yukon Gold potatoes, diced (about 1 pound)
- 2 cups canned corn kernels, divided
- 4 cups homemade (onion- and garlic-free) vegetable broth
- 1 teaspoon ground cumin
- ½ teaspoon smoked paprika
- ⅛ teaspoon cayenne
- 1 teaspoon salt
- 1 cup rice milk
- 3 scallions, green parts only, thinly sliced

Directions:

1.   Heat the olive oil and Garlic Oil in a stockpot over medium heat. Add the celery and carrots and cook, stirring occasionally, for about 5 minutes, until the vegetables begin to soften. Add the leek, red bell peppers, potatoes, 1 cup of the corn, broth, cumin, smoked paprika, cayenne, and salt, and bring to a boil. Reduce the heat to low and simmer for about 30 minutes, until the potatoes are very tender.

2.   Using an immersion blender or in batches in a countertop blender, purée the soup.

3.   Stir in the remaining cup of corn and the rice milk, and cook over low heat for about 10 minutes more, until the soup is heated through and the corn kernels are tender. Serve immediately, garnished with sliced scallions.

Nutrition Info:

- InfoCalories: 355; Protein: 13g; Total Fat: 7g; Saturated Fat: 1g; Carbohydrates: 69g; Fiber: 8g; Sodium: 1416mg;

Crustless Spinach Quiche

Servings:4
Cooking Time: 20 Minutes
Ingredients:

- Nonstick cooking spray
- 6 eggs, beaten
- ¼ cup unsweetened almond milk
- ½ teaspoon sea salt
- ⅛ teaspoon freshly ground black pepper
- 1 teaspoon dried thyme
- 2 cups (2 [8-ounce] boxes) frozen spinach, thawed and squeezed of excess moisture
- ½ cup grated Swiss cheese

Directions:

1.   Preheat the oven to 350°F.
2.   Spray a 9-inch pie pan with nonstick cooking spray.
3.   In a medium bowl, whisk together the eggs, almond milk, salt, pepper, and thyme.
4.   Fold in the spinach and cheese. Pour the mixture into the prepared pie pan.
5.   Bake for 20 to 25 minutes, until the quiche sets.

Nutrition Info:

- InfoCalories:187; Total Fat: 14g; Saturated Fat: 8g; Carbohydrates: 3g; Fiber: <1g; Sodium: 368mg; Protein: 13g

Vegetable Fried Rice

Servings:2
Cooking Time:x
Ingredients:

- 2 large eggs
- 1 tablespoon sesame oil
- 1/2 medium carrot, peeled and thinly sliced
- 1/2 medium red bell pepper, seeded and diced
- 1 teaspoon palm sugar
- 1/16 teaspoon wheat-free asafetida powder
- 1 tablespoon gluten-free soy sauce (tamari)
- 1 teaspoon gluten-free fish sauce
- 1 tablespoon rice wine vinegar
- 1 large green onion, chopped, green part only
- 1 tablespoon freshly grated gingerroot
- 1 cup cooked brown rice
- 2 cups baby spinach

Directions:

1. Whisk eggs in a small bowl. Heat a wok or medium skillet on medium-high; spray with cooking spray and add eggs to pan. Cook 4–5 minutes or until eggs are cooked but still slightly moist. Set eggs aside on cutting board.
2. Add sesame oil to pan, then add carrot and bell pepper. Cook about 3 minutes, stirring occasionally.
3. Meanwhile, in a small bowl, stir together sugar, asafetida, soy sauce, fish sauce, and vinegar until sugar is dissolved.
4. Add green onion to pan and stir 1 minute; add ginger and cook 1 more minute.
5. Add rice and cook 2 minutes, stirring. Add soy sauce mixture and continue stirring until absorbed into rice, about 2 minutes.
6. Add spinach and cook until wilted, about 3 minutes. Coarsely chop egg and stir into rice.

Nutrition Info:

- InfoCalories: 296,Fat: 13g,Protein: 11g,Sodium: 790mg,Carbohydrates: 35.

Pineapple Fried Rice

Servings:4
Cooking Time: 10 Minutes
Ingredients:

- 2 tablespoons Garlic Oil
- 6 scallions, green parts only, finely chopped
- 1/2 cup canned water chestnuts, drained
- 1 tablespoon peeled and grated fresh ginger
- 3 cups cooked brown rice
- 2 cups canned pineapple (in juice), drained, 1/4 cup juice reserved
- 2 tablespoons gluten-free soy sauce
- 1/4 cup chopped fresh cilantro leaves

Directions:

1. In a large skillet over medium-high heat, heat the garlic oil until it shimmers.
2. Add the scallions, water chestnuts, and ginger. Cook for 5 minutes, stirring.
3. Add the brown rice, pineapple, reserved pineapple juice, and soy sauce. Cook for 5 minutes, stirring, until the rice is warmed through.
4. Stir in the cilantro.

Nutrition Info:

- InfoCalories:413; Total Fat: 9g; Saturated Fat: 1g; Carbohydrates: 77g; Fiber: 4g; Sodium: 396mg; Protein: 7g

Goat Cheese And Potato Tacos With Red Chili Cream Sauce

Servings:4
Cooking Time:x
Ingredients:

- 2 white potatoes, peeled
- 1 teaspoon salt, divided
- 1 small red chili, seeded and sliced
- 1 (6-ounce) container lactose-free plain yogurt
- 1 teaspoon light brown sugar
- 1 tablespoon lemon juice
- 1½ teaspoons chili powder
- 1 teaspoon ground cumin
- ¼ teaspoon freshly ground black pepper
- 1 tablespoon coconut oil
- 1 (10-ounce) package frozen corn, thawed
- 8 (6") corn tortillas, warmed
- ¾ cup crumbled goat cheese
- ¼ cup finely chopped fresh cilantro
- ½ medium avocado, cut into 4 slices

Directions:

1. Preheat oven to 400°F.
2. In a medium saucepot, cover potatoes with cold water. Add ½ teaspoon salt and bring to a boil. Cook at a rolling boil about 20–30 minutes or until a fork can be inserted fully into potatoes. Drain and set aside to cool.
3. For the chili sauce: Blend chili, yogurt, brown sugar, and lemon juice in a small blender or food processor. Sauce should be pinkish-red in color. Set aside.
4. Cut potatoes into ¾" chunks and add to a medium bowl. Add chili powder, cumin, remaining salt, and pepper. Toss to combine.
5. Add coconut oil to a medium skillet over medium-high heat. Add potatoes and toss until golden brown, turning occasionally, about 10 minutes. Set aside in bowl.
6. Add corn to skillet and cook 2 minutes.
7. Fill tortillas with potatoes, corn, goat cheese, and cilantro.
8. Serve with avocado and red chili cream sauce.

Nutrition Info:

- InfoCalories: 538,Fat: 26g,Protein: 22g,Sodium: 799mg,Carbohydrates: 61.

Turmeric Rice With Cranberries

Servings:2
Cooking Time:x
Ingredients:

- ½ cup no-sugar-added dried cranberries
- 2 cups lukewarm water
- 1 tablespoon coconut oil
- 2 tablespoons pine nuts
- ½ teaspoon ground turmeric
- 1/16 teaspoon wheat-free asafetida powder
- ½ teaspoon saffron dissolved in ¼ cup hot water
- 2 tablespoons light brown sugar
- ¼ teaspoon sea salt
- 1 cup cooked basmati rice

Directions:

1. Soak cranberries in lukewarm water for about 10 minutes to plump. Drain.
2. In a wok or medium skillet on medium-high, heat coconut oil and stir in cranberries and pine nuts. Add turmeric, asafetida, saffron, sugar, and salt and reduce heat to low; cook 7 minutes.
3. Add rice and stir until evenly coated; serve immediately.

Nutrition Info:

- InfoCalories: 396,Fat: 16g,Protein: 4g,Sodium: 307mg,Carbohydrates: 63.

Mac 'n' Cheeze

Servings:4
Cooking Time:x
Ingredients:

- 1 pound brown rice pasta noodles
- 3 tablespoons nutritional yeast
- 1⁄2 teaspoon sea salt, divided
- 1⁄4 cup coconut oil
- 1⁄4 cup sweet rice flour
- 23⁄4 cups unsweetened almond milk
- 1 teaspoon rice wine vinegar
- 1⁄2 cup dairy-free cheese shreds
- 1⁄4 teaspoon freshly ground black pepper
- 1 teaspoon paprika

Directions:

1. Bring a large pot of salted water to a rolling boil and cook pasta until al dente according to package directions. Drain and set aside.
2. In a small bowl, combine yeast and 1⁄4 teaspoon sea salt. Set aside.
3. In a large skillet, heat coconut oil over medium-low heat. Whisk in flour and continue whisking constantly 3–5 minutes or until flour smells toasty but hasn't browned.
4. In a steady stream, whisk in almond milk, stirring constantly. Add yeast mixture and vinegar. Cook 3 minutes or until slightly thickened.
5. Add cheese shreds and mix until well incorporated.
6. Add pasta and toss with sauce, black pepper, and remaining salt. Cook 1–2 minutes more to reheat pasta. Sprinkle on paprika. Serve immediately.

Nutrition Info:

- InfoCalories: 574,Fat: 16g,Protein: 13g,Sodium: 646mg,Carbohydrates: 91.

Coconut-curry Tofu With Vegetables

Servings:4
Cooking Time: 25 Minutes
Ingredients:

- FOR THE SAUCE
- 1 cup canned coconut milk
- 2 tablespoons chopped fresh cilantro
- 1 tablespoon gluten-free, onion- and garlic-free curry powder
- 1 teaspoon brown sugar
- 1 teaspoon salt
- FOR THE TOFU AND VEGETABLES
- 1 tablespoon grapeseed oil
- 14 ounces extra-firm tofu, drained and cut into cubes
- 1 red bell pepper, sliced
- 1 zucchini, halved lengthwise and sliced
- 2 cups broccoli florets
- 1 bunch baby bok choy, cut into 2-inch pieces

Directions:

1. To make the sauce, in a small bowl, stir together the coconut milk, cilantro, curry powder, brown sugar, and salt.
2. To prepare the tofu and vegetables, heat the oil in a large skillet over high heat. Arrange the tofu in the pan in a single layer and cook, without stirring, for about 5 minutes, until it begins to brown on the bottom. Scrape the tofu from the pan with a spatula and continue to cook, stirring occasionally, until it is golden brown all over, for about 7 more minutes.
3. Add the bell pepper, zucchini, broccoli, and bok choy to the pan, along with the sauce mixture, and continue to cook, stirring, for about 8 to 10 minutes, until the vegetables are tender. Serve immediately.

Nutrition Info:

- InfoCalories: 321; Protein: 16g; Total Fat: 25g; Saturated Fat: 14g; Carbohydrates: 17g; Fiber: 6g; Sodium: 756mg;

Vegetable Stir-fry

Servings:4
Cooking Time: 10 Minutes
Ingredients:

- 2 tablespoons Garlic Oil
- 2⅔ cups chopped firm tofu
- 8 scallions, green parts only, chopped
- 2 cups broccoli florets
- ½ cup Stir-Fry Sauce

Directions:

1. In a large skillet over medium-high heat, heat the garlic oil until it shimmers.
2. Add the tofu, scallions, and broccoli. Cook for about 7 minutes, stirring frequently, until the broccoli is crisp-tender.
3. Stir in the stir-fry sauce. Cook for about 3 minutes, stirring, until it thickens.

Nutrition Info:

- InfoCalories:231; Total Fat: 14g; Saturated Fat: 3g; Carbohydrates: 14g; Fiber: 4g; Sodium: 426mg; Protein: 16g

Tofu Burger Patties

Servings:4
Cooking Time: 10 Minutes
Ingredients:

- 8 ounces firm tofu, mashed with a fork
- 4 scallions, green parts only, minced
- 1 cup rolled oats
- 1 egg, beaten
- 2 teaspoons ground cumin
- 2 teaspoons chili powder
- ½ teaspoon sea salt
- ¼ teaspoon freshly ground black pepper
- Nonstick cooking spray

Directions:

1. In a medium bowl, stir together the tofu, scallions, oats, egg, cumin, chili powder, salt, and pepper. Form the mixture into 4 patties.
2. Spray a large nonstick skillet with cooking spray and place it over medium-high heat.
3. Add the patties and cook for about 5 minutes per side, until browned on both sides.

Nutrition Info:

- InfoCalories:146; Total Fat: 5g; Saturated Fat: 1g; Carbohydrates: 17g; Fiber: 4g; Sodium: 275mg; Protein: 10g

Tempeh Tacos

Servings:4
Cooking Time:x
Ingredients:

- 1 (8-ounce) package tempeh
- 2 small vine-ripe tomatoes, chopped
- 1 teaspoon chili powder
- ½ teaspoon ground cumin
- 3 tablespoons lime juice, divided
- 2–4 tablespoons water
- 1½ tablespoons coconut oil, divided
- ½ medium green bell pepper, seeded and diced
- 2 cups common (green) cabbage, diced
- 8 (6") soft corn tortillas, warmed
- 1½ cups Fiesta Salsa (see recipe in Chapter 13)
- ½ medium avocado, cut into eighths

Directions:

1. Crumble tempeh into a large mixing bowl. Add tomatoes, chili powder, cumin, and 1 tablespoon lime juice. Stir in 1 tablespoon water and mix again. If tempeh mixture seems a little dry, add more water. Set aside.
2. Heat 1 tablespoon oil in large skillet over medium-high heat. Add bell pepper and cabbage. Cook for 10–12 minutes, stirring occasionally.
3. Add tempeh mixture and cook 8–10 minutes, stirring frequently. Halfway through cooking, add 1 tablespoon lime juice, 1 tablespoon water, and ½ tablespoon coconut oil. Add 2 more tablespoons of water and 1 tablespoon lime juice toward end of cooking. Stir again. Remove from heat. Mixture should be moist. Add more water if necessary.
4. Fill tortillas with tempeh mixture, salsa, and cabbage, and top with avocado.

Nutrition Info:

- InfoCalories: 472,Fat: 24g,Protein: 19g,Sodium: 992mg,Carbohydrates: 52.

Mediterranean Noodles

Servings:4
Cooking Time:x
Ingredients:

- 1 medium eggplant
- 1/2 cup garlic-infused olive oil
- 1/2 teaspoon sea salt
- 2 teaspoons freshly ground black pepper
- 1 (12-ounce) package gluten-free fusilli, cooked, drained, and rinsed under cold water
- 20 grape tomatoes, halved
- 1/2 cup sliced black olives
- 20 fresh basil leaves, torn
- 1 teaspoon dried oregano
- Juice of 2 medium lemons
- 1/2 cup grated Parmesan cheese

Directions:

1. Preheat oven to 475°F.
2. Cut eggplant into chunks and place in a large bowl. Using your hands, toss eggplant with oil, salt, and black pepper.
3. Place eggplant in a single layer on a baking sheet. Bake 20 minutes, flipping halfway through baking. When done, remove from oven and allow to cool. Eggplant should be soft. Transfer back to large bowl along with cooked noodles.
4. Stir in tomatoes, olives, basil, oregano, lemon juice, and Parmesan and serve.

Nutrition Info:

- InfoCalories: 470,Fat: 33g,Protein: 11g,Sodium: 680mg,Carbohydrates: 36.

Tempeh Coconut Curry Bowls

Servings:2
Cooking Time:x
Ingredients:

- 1 tablespoon canola oil
- 1/2 teaspoon ground turmeric
- 1/2 teaspoon ground coriander
- 1 teaspoon mustard seeds
- 1/2 teaspoon cayenne pepper
- 1 tablespoon minced fresh gingerroot
- 2 tablespoons fresh minced lemongrass
- 2 tablespoons red curry paste
- 1/16 teaspoon salt
- 1 pound Yukon Gold potatoes, peeled and cut into small cubes (about 3 cups)
- 1 cup water
- 1 (13.5-ounce) can light coconut milk
- 8 ounces tempeh, cut into 3/4" cubes
- 2 teaspoons gluten-free soy sauce (tamari)
- 1/2 tablespoon fresh lime juice
- 1/2 tablespoon fresh lemon juice
- 1 cup uncooked basmati rice
- 1/4 cup shredded unsweetened coconut

Directions:

1. Heat oil in a large nonstick skillet over medium-high heat. Add turmeric, coriander, mustard seeds, cayenne pepper, ginger, lemongrass, and curry paste; cook 4 minutes, stirring frequently.
2. Add salt, potatoes, water, coconut milk, and tempeh; bring to a boil. Cover, reduce heat, and simmer 15 minutes or until potatoes are tender.
3. Stir in soy sauce and lemon and lime juices. Simmer uncovered 5 minutes.
4. Cook rice according to package instructions. Once rice is done, add coconut shreds. Serve with curry in bowls.

Nutrition Info:

- InfoCalories: 648,Fat: 42g,Protein: 21g,Sodium: 631mg,Carbohydrates: 54.

Tofu And Red Bell Pepper Quinoa

Servings:4
Cooking Time: 21 Minutes
Ingredients:
- Rest: 5 minutes
- 2 tablespoons Garlic Oil
- 1 red bell pepper, chopped
- 6 ounces firm tofu, chopped
- 1 cup quinoa, rinsed well
- 2 cups Low-FODMAP Vegetable Broth
- 1 teaspoon dried thyme
- ½ teaspoon sea salt
- ¼ teaspoon freshly ground black pepper

Directions:
1. In a large saucepan over medium-high heat, heat the garlic oil until it shimmers.
2. Add the bell pepper and the tofu. Cook for about 5 minutes, stirring, until the pepper is soft.
3. Add the quinoa. Cook for 1 minute, stirring.
4. Add the broth, thyme, salt, and pepper. Bring to a boil. Reduce the heat to medium and simmer for 15 minutes.
5. Turn off the heat. Cover the pot and let it sit for 5 minutes more.
6. Fluff with a fork.

Nutrition Info:
- InfoCalories:276; Total Fat: 12g; Saturated Fat: 2g; Carbohydrates: 31g; Fiber: 4g; Sodium: 624mg; Protein: 12g

Baked Tofu And Vegetables

Servings:4
Cooking Time:x
Ingredients:
- 2 (14-ounce) packages extra-firm tofu, pressed between paper towels and patted dry
- 2 tablespoons toasted sesame oil, divided
- 2 teaspoons sesame seeds
- 2 1/2 tablespoons gluten-free soy sauce (tamari), divided
- 7–8 cups chopped bok choy (about 8 stalks)
- 1 bunch scallions, diced, green part only
- 1 medium red bell pepper, seeded and diced
- 1/4 cup slivered almonds
- 2 tablespoons rice wine vinegar

Directions:
1. Preheat oven to 400°F. Grease a large rimmed baking sheet with cooking spray.
2. Cut tofu into 1" pieces and toss in a large bowl with 1 tablespoon sesame oil, sesame seeds, and 2 tablespoons soy sauce.
3. Spread in a single layer on the prepared baking sheet. Bake tofu on lower rack of oven. Bake until browned, 25–30 minutes, flipping once.
4. While tofu is baking, heat a large skillet on medium-high and coat with 1 tablespoon sesame oil.
5. Add bok choy, scallions, bell pepper, almonds, remaining 1/2 tablespoon soy sauce, and vinegar. Cook until bok choy is slightly tender, stirring frequently. Place in same bowl used to prepare tofu.
6. Once tofu is ready, add to vegetables in bowl and stir until combined. Divide into 4 bowls and serve.

Nutrition Info:
- InfoCalories: 267,Fat: 16g,Protein: 18g,Sodium: 725mg,Carbohydrates: 12.

Vegan Pad Thai

Servings:2
Cooking Time:x
Ingredients:

- 2 1⁄2 cups water, divided
- 1 (10-ounce) package rice noodles or ramen-style noodles
- 2 tablespoons peanut butter
- Juice of 2 medium limes
- 3 tablespoons palm sugar
- 1 chili (about 4" long), chopped and seeded
- 4 tablespoons gluten-free soy sauce (tamari), divided
- 2 tablespoons garlic-infused olive oil
- 1⁄2 (12-ounce package) extra-firm tofu, drained and cut into cubes
- 1 medium head broccoli, florets chopped small
- 2 cups bean sprouts
- 1 large scallion, green part only
- 2 tablespoons chopped unsalted peanuts

Directions:

1. Bring 1 1⁄2 cups water to boil in a medium pot and submerge noodles to soak. Turn off heat.
2. In a small bowl, whisk together peanut butter, lime juice, sugar, chili, 3 tablespoons soy sauce, and 1 cup water.
3. In a large frying pan, heat oil on medium and add tofu. Drizzle 1 tablespoon soy sauce over tofu and sauté until golden brown. Add broccoli and bean sprouts. Cook 4–5 minutes.
4. Drain noodles. Add peanut butter mixture and stir well. Add to tofu and cook through, about 5 minutes.
5. Garnish with scallions and peanuts. Serve immediately.

Nutrition Info:

- InfoCalories: 454,Fat: 13g,Protein: 16g,Sodium: 920mg,Carbohydrates: 73.

Soups, Salads And Sides Recipes

Mussels In Chili, Bacon, And Tomato Broth

Servings:4
Cooking Time:x
Ingredients:

- 4 ounces (113 g) lean bacon slices, cut crosswise into thin strips
- 2 tablespoons olive oil
- 3 cups (750 ml) tomato puree
- ½ teaspoon cayenne pepper (or to taste)
- 6½ cups (1.5 liters) reduced sodium gluten-free, onion-free chicken stock*
- 5½ pounds (2.5 kg) mussels, scrubbed and debearded
- Salt and freshly ground black pepper
- Gluten-free bread, for serving

Directions:

1. In a large heavy-bottomed saucepan over medium heat, cook the bacon until just golden. Spoon out and discard any excess fat, then add the olive oil, tomato puree, cayenne, and 2 cups (500 ml) of the stock. Bring to a boil, reduce the heat to low, and simmer for 30 to 40 minutes to develop the smoky bacon flavor.
2. Add the remaining stock. Increase the heat to medium-high and bring to a boil. Add the mussels and cook, covered, for 5 to 8 minutes, until all the mussels have opened. Shake the pan to redistribute the mussels and cook for an extra minute. Shake again. Discard any unopened mussels. Season to taste with salt and pepper and serve immediately with plenty of gluten-free bread to mop up the delicious broth.

Nutrition Info:

- Info: 612 calories,59 g protein,26 g total fat,33 g carbohydrates,2082 mg sodiu.

Spinach And Bell Pepper Salad With Fried Tofu Puffs

Servings:4
Cooking Time:x
Ingredients:

- ¼ cup (60 ml) gluten-free soy sauce
- ¼ cup (60 ml) fresh lemon juice
- 1 tablespoon plus 1 teaspoon seasoned rice vinegar
- ¼ cup (55 g) packed light brown sugar
- ¼ cup (60 ml) sesame oil
- 10½ ounces (300 g) baby spinach leaves (10 cups), rinsed and dried
- 1½ cups (75 g) snow pea shoots or bean sprouts
- 1 green bell pepper, seeded and sliced
- 14 ounces (400 g) fried tofu puffs, cut into cubes
- ⅓ cup (50 g) pine nuts
- Salt and freshly ground black pepper

Directions:

1. Combine the soy sauce, lemon juice, vinegar, brown sugar, and sesame oil in a small bowl and whisk well.
2. Toss the spinach, snow pea shoots, bell pepper, tofu, and pine nuts in a large bowl until well combined. Drizzle with the dressing and toss briefly. Season to taste with salt and pepper and serve.

Nutrition Info:

- Info: 571 calories,24 g protein,40 g total fat,40 g carbohydrates,1054 mg sodiu.

Fennel Pomegranate Salad

Servings:2
Cooking Time:x

Ingredients:

- 3 small fennel bulbs, thinly sliced
- 1/4 medium stalk celery, sliced into thin slivers
- 1/2 cup coarsely chopped fresh parsley
- 1/2 cup pomegranate seeds, divided
- 1/4 cup fresh lemon juice
- 1/4 cup extra-virgin olive oil
- 1/4 teaspoon salt
- 1/2 teaspoon freshly ground black pepper
- 1/2 cup crumbled goat cheese

Directions:

1. Toss fennel, celery, parsley, and 1/4 cup pomegranate seeds in a large bowl.
2. Add lemon juice and oil and toss to coat. Add salt and pepper.
3. Serve topped with goat cheese and remaining pomegranate seeds.

Nutrition Info:

- InfoCalories: 394,Fat: 30g,Protein: 12g,Sodium: 400mg,Carbohydrates: 23.

Filet Mignon Salad

Servings:2
Cooking Time:x

Ingredients:

- 1/4 large head romaine lettuce, chopped (stems removed)
- 1/2 large head Belgian endive (about 1 1/2 cups), thinly sliced crosswise
- 1/4 cup chopped fresh basil
- 1 1/2 cups baby arugula
- 2 teaspoons maple syrup
- 1/2 cup rice wine vinegar
- 1 1/2 tablespoons lemon juice
- 1/2 teaspoon sea salt
- 1/2 teaspoon freshly ground black pepper
- 1/2 cup plus 1/2 tablespoon olive oil
- 1 tablespoon unsalted butter
- 1/2 pound filet mignon
- 2 ounces crumbled goat cheese
- 8 cherry tomatoes, halved

Directions:

1. In a large salad bowl combine romaine, endive, basil, and arugula.
2. In a food processor or blender, add maple syrup, vinegar, lemon juice, salt, and pepper. With machine running on low speed, slowly blend in 1/2 cup oil. Set aside.
3. Melt butter with 1/2 tablespoon olive oil in a medium cast-iron skillet or stainless steel skillet over medium heat. Add filet mignon and cook 5–7 minutes on each side or longer depending on desired degree of doneness. Allow to stand 5 minutes. Slice into strips of medium thickness.
4. Add filet mignon, goat cheese, and cherry tomatoes to salad bowl. Pour in dressing. Toss well to coat, and serve.

Nutrition Info:

- InfoCalories: 449,Fat: 45g,Protein: 16g,Sodium: 381mg,Carbohydrates: 6.

Orange-maple Glazed Carrots

Servings:4
Cooking Time:20 Minutes
Ingredients:
- 2 tablespoons pure maple syrup
- 1 tablespoon extra-virgin olive oil
- Juice of 1 orange
- Zest of 1 orange
- ½ teaspoon sea salt
- ¼ teaspoon freshly ground black pepper
- 2 cups baby carrots

Directions:
1. Preheat the oven to 400°F.
2. Line a baking sheet with parchment paper and set it aside.
3. In a medium bowl, whisk together the maple syrup, olive oil, orange juice, orange zest, salt, and pepper.
4. Add the carrots and toss to coat.
5. Spread the carrots in a single layer on the prepared sheet. Roast for 20 minutes, or until browned.

Nutrition Info:
- InfoCalories: 101,Total Fat: 4g,Carbohydrates: 17g,Sodium: 298mg,Protein: 1.

Veggie Dip

Servings: 16
Cooking Time:5 Minutes
Ingredients:
- 1 cup mayonnaise
- 2 cups Greek yogurt
- 2 cups kale, chopped finely
- 1 ½ cups bell peppers, variety of colors, chopped finely
- 2 cups water chestnuts, chopped finely
- 3 spring onions, green parts only, chopped finely
- 1 tsp garlic-infused oil
- Pinch of salt
- Fresh sliced vegetables and corn chips for serving

Directions:
1. In a bowl, mix all the ingredients well, except for the fresh sliced vegetables. Place in the fridge until serving.
2. Serve with the fresh vegetables.

Nutrition Info:
- Info123g Cal,10 g Fat ,3 g Carbs ,3 g Protein.

Caprese Salad

Servings:4
Cooking Time:0 Minutes
Ingredients:
- 2 cups torn romaine lettuce
- 20 cherry tomatoes, quartered
- ¼ cup loosely packed fresh basil leaves, chopped
- 4 ounces mozzarella cheese, chopped
- ¼ cup Italian Basil Vinaigrette

Directions:
1. In a large bowl, combine the lettuce, tomatoes, basil, and cheese.
2. Add the vinaigrette and toss to coat.

Nutrition Info:
- InfoCalories: 265,Total Fat: 14g,Carbohydrates: 26g,Sodium: 202mg,Protein: 14.

Caramelized Squash Salad With Sun-dried Tomatoes And Basil

Servings:4
Cooking Time:x
Ingredients:
- 2 pounds 10 ounces (1.2 kg) kabocha or other suitable winter squash, peeled, seeded, and cut into ¾-inch (2 cm) cubes
- 1 eggplant, cut into ¼-inch (5 mm) slices
- ¼ cup (60 ml) olive oil
- 12 or 13 pieces (50 g) sun-dried tomatoes in oil, drained and sliced
- ½ cup (100 g) thawed frozen corn kernels
- Small handful of basil leaves, roughly chopped

Directions:
1. Preheat the oven to 350°F (180°C).
2. Spread the squash and eggplant on two separate baking sheets and brush with 2 tablespoons of the olive oil. Bake for 25 minutes or until tender and golden brown. Let cool to room temperature, then roughly chop the eggplant.
3. Combine the squash, eggplant, sun-dried tomatoes, corn, basil, and the remaining 2 tablespoons of olive oil in a large bowl. Refrigerate for 2 to 3 hours to allow the flavors to develop. Bring to room temperature before serving.

Nutrition Info:
- Info: 288 calories,5 g protein,15 g total fat,41 g carbohydrates,148 mg sodiu.

Roasted Potato Wedges

Servings:4
Cooking Time:30 Minutes
Ingredients:
- 1 pound Yukon Gold potatoes, quartered lengthwise
- 2 tablespoons Garlic Oil
- 1 tablespoon chopped fresh rosemary leaves
- ½ teaspoon sea salt
- ¼ teaspoon freshly ground black pepper

Directions:
1. Preheat the oven to 425°F.
2. In a large bowl, toss the potatoes with the garlic oil, rosemary, salt, and pepper. Divide them between two baking sheets and spread into a single layer.
3. Bake for about 30 minutes until the potatoes are browned. Stir them once or twice and rotate the pans (switching racks) halfway through cooking.

Nutrition Info:
- InfoCalories: 143,Total Fat: 7g,Carbohydrates: 19g,Sodium: 241mg,Protein: 2.

Chopped Italian Salad

Servings:4
Cooking Time:0 Minutes
Ingredients:
- 4 cups chopped romaine lettuce
- 8 cherry tomatoes, halved
- 1 medium zucchini, chopped
- 1 cup black olives, halved
- ¼ cup Italian Balsamic Vinaigrette

Directions:
1. In a medium bowl, combine the lettuce, tomatoes, zucchini, and olives.
2. Add the vinaigrette and toss to coat.

Nutrition Info:
- InfoCalories: 158,Total Fat: 10g,Carbohydrates: 16g,Sodium: 433mg,Protein: 3.

Glorious Strawberry Salad

Servings:4
Cooking Time:x
Ingredients:

- 6 cups fresh baby spinach
- 1/2 cup sliced strawberries
- 1/4 cup whole walnuts
- 1/4 cup chopped fresh basil
- 1/2 cup crumbled goat cheese
- 1/4 teaspoon sea salt
- 1 tablespoon freshly ground black pepper
- 3 tablespoons rice wine vinegar
- 2/3 cup extra-virgin olive oil
- 1/2 medium avocado, cut into eighths

Directions:

1. In a large salad bowl toss together spinach, strawberries, walnuts, basil, goat cheese, salt, and pepper.
2. In a small bowl whisk together vinegar and oil. Drizzle over salad and toss salad again.
3. Serve on individual salad plates and top each with avocado.

Nutrition Info:

- InfoCalories: 478,Fat: 48g,Protein: 6g,Sodium: 396mg,Carbohydrates: 8.

Mashed Potatoes

Servings: 14 (½ Cup Each)
Cooking Time:15 Minutes
Ingredients:

- 4 large Russet potatoes
- 1 tbsp rosemary, fresh, chopped
- 2 tbsp butter or margarine
- 2 tbsp olive oil
- ½ cup feta cheese
- ½ cup lactose-free milk
- Pinch of salt

Directions:

1. Wash and peel the potatoes, then cut into cubes. Place them into a pot and cover with water. Add a little extra water to allow for evaporation. Cover the pot and bring the water to a boil, then lower the heat, remove the lid, and cook until the potatoes feel tender when poked with a fork. Carefully pour out the water and leave open for 5 minutes.
2. While the potatoes are cooking, chop the rosemary.
3. After the five minutes, add the ingredients, except the salt and rosemary, to the pot and mash the ingredients together until you reach the desired consistency. Add rosemary and salt to taste.

Nutrition Info:

- Info106g Cal,5 g Fat ,11 g Carbs ,3 g Protein.

Bacon Mashed Potatoes

Servings:4
Cooking Time: 15 Minutes
Ingredients:

- 1 pound new or baby potatoes, cut into 1-inch cubes
- 2 slices bacon
- 1/3 cup lactose-free milk
- ½ teaspoon salt
- ¼ teaspoon freshly ground black pepper
- ¼ cup unsalted butter
- 4 scallions, green parts only, sliced

Directions:

1. Put the potatoes in a large saucepan, cover with 2 inches of water, and bring to a boil over medium-high heat. Lower the heat to medium and cook for 10 to 12 minutes, until the potatoes are tender. Drain the potatoes and place them in a large bowl.
2. While the potatoes are cooking, cook the bacon in a large skillet over medium heat for about 4 minutes per side, until browned and crisp. Drain on paper towels, and then crumble.
3. In the large bowl, mash the potatoes with a potato masher. Add the milk, salt, pepper, and butter. Continue mashing until the potatoes are smooth, the butter is melted, and everything is well mixed. Stir in the bacon and scallions. Serve immediately.

Nutrition Info:

- InfoCalories: 203; Protein: 5g; Total Fat: 14g; Saturated Fat: 8g; Carbohydrates: 16g; Fiber: 3g; Sodium: 479mg;

Kale Sesame Salad With Tamari-ginger Dressing

Servings:2

Cooking Time:x

Ingredients:

- 1 1⁄2 tablespoons sesame seeds
- 4 cups shredded kale (thick ribs and stems removed)
- 3 tablespoons extra-virgin olive oil, divided
- 1 tablespoon chopped scallion, green part only
- 1⁄2 cup peeled and julienned carrots
- 1 tablespoon rice wine vinegar
- 1⁄2 tablespoon finely grated gingerroot
- 1⁄2 tablespoon gluten-free soy sauce (tamari)
- 1 teaspoon lime juice
- 1⁄16 teaspoon wheat-free asafetida powder
- 1⁄4 medium avocado, sliced in half
- 2 tablespoons chopped fresh basil

Directions:

1. Using a small skillet set over medium-high heat, toast sesame seeds until golden brown, about 1 minute. Stir continuously to keep seeds from burning. Set aside.
2. Place kale in a large salad bowl. Add 1 tablespoon olive oil and massage with hands until kale leaves become soft. Add scallion and carrots and toss to combine.
3. Make dressing in a small bowl by whisking together vinegar, ginger, soy sauce, lime juice, and asafetida.
4. Pour dressing over kale and stir again to combine. Divide into 2 salad bowls and top each with sesame seeds, 1 slice avocado, and 1 tablespoon basil.

Nutrition Info:

- InfoCalories: 344,Fat: 28g,Protein: 7g,Sodium: 306mg,Carbohydrates: 21.

Quinoa With Swiss Chard

Servings:4

Cooking Time: 25 Minutes

Ingredients:

- 1 tablespoon Garlic Oil (here)
- 1 bunch Swiss chard, stems removed and leaves julienned
- 1 teaspoon ground cumin
- 1 teaspoon ground coriander
- 2 teaspoons paprika
- 1⁄2 teaspoon salt
- 1 cup quinoa
- 2 cups homemade (onion- and garlic-free) vegetable broth

Directions:

1. Heat the oil in a large skillet set over medium heat. Add the Swiss chard, cumin, coriander, paprika, salt, quinoa, and broth and bring to a boil.
2. Cover, reduce the heat to low, and cook for 20 minutes, until the liquid has evaporated and the quinoa is tender. Serve hot.

Nutrition Info:

- InfoCalories: 207; Protein: 9g; Total Fat: 7g; Saturated Fat: 1g; Carbohydrates: 29g; Fiber: 4g; Sodium: 753mg;

Turkey And Brown Rice Soup

Servings:6
Cooking Time:x
Ingredients:

- 1 cup brown rice, rinsed
- 2 tablespoons extra-virgin olive oil
- 4 medium carrots, peeled and sliced into 1/4" rounds
- 1 medium red bell pepper, seeded and diced
- 1 bay leaf
- 6 cups Basic Roast Chicken Stock (see recipe in this chapter)
- 1 (14.5-ounce) can of diced tomatoes
- 4 (3-ounce) turkey breast cutlets (uncooked), cut into 1" squares
- 5 cups baby spinach leaves
- 2 tablespoons chopped fresh flat-leaf parsley
- 1/8 teaspoon sea salt
- 1/8 teaspoon freshly ground black pepper

Directions:

1. Cook rice in a saucepan or rice cooker according to package directions.
2. Heat olive oil in a stockpot over medium-high heat. Add carrots, bell pepper, and bay leaf. Sauté 5 minutes, stirring occasionally.
3. Add stock, tomatoes, and turkey to soup pot. Bring to a boil, then turn down heat and simmer, uncovered, for 45 minutes, stirring occasionally.
4. Remove bay leaf and stir in spinach until wilted.
5. Turn off heat. Stir in rice, parsley, salt, and pepper.

Nutrition Info:

- InfoCalories: 345,Fat: 9g,Protein: 28g,Sodium: 325mg,Carbohydrates: 33.

Lentil Chili

Servings:4
Cooking Time:x
Ingredients:

- 1 tablespoon olive oil
- 1 medium stalk celery, diced
- 1 large carrot, peeled and diced, or 1 cup store-bought shredded carrots
- 1 large red bell pepper, seeded and chopped
- 4 cups Vegetable Stock (see recipe in this chapter)
- 2 teaspoons chili powder
- 1 teaspoon ground cumin
- 2 cups canned lentils, drained and thoroughly rinsed
- 3 Roma tomatoes, diced
- 1/4 cup chopped fresh cilantro
- 2 cups baby spinach
- 1/2 cup lactose-free sour cream (optional)

Directions:

1. Heat a large pot over medium-high heat and add olive oil.
2. Once hot, add celery, carrot, and bell pepper; sauté about 5 minutes, stirring frequently.
3. Stir in 1/4 cup stock.
4. Add chili powder and cumin and stir; cook 1 minute.
5. Add lentils, tomatoes, cilantro, and remaining stock. Once boiling, reduce heat to medium-low and simmer 25 minutes partially covered.
6. Uncover and cook 8 minutes longer. Add spinach and stir, cooking another 2 minutes.
7. Top with sour cream if using and serve.

Nutrition Info:

- InfoCalories: 236,Fat: 8g,Protein: 12g,Sodium: 614mg,Carbohydrates: 32.

Caramelized Fennel

Servings:4
Cooking Time: 60 Minutes
Ingredients:

- ¼ cup olive oil
- 4 large fennel bulbs, cut into ¼-inch-thick slices
- 1 teaspoon salt
- ¼ cup freshly grated Parmesan
- 2 tablespoons chopped fresh parsley
- 1 teaspoon lemon zest
- 2 teaspoons lemon juice

Directions:

1. In a large, heavy skillet, heat the olive oil over medium-high heat. Stir in the fennel and salt, reduce the heat to medium, and cook, stirring occasionally, for 45 to 60 minutes, lowering the heat if needed, until the fennel is golden brown and very tender.
2. Just before serving, stir in the cheese, parsley, lemon zest, and lemon juice.

Nutrition Info:

- InfoCalories: 228; Protein: 8g; Total Fat: 16g; Saturated Fat: 4g; Carbohydrates: 18g; Fiber: 7g; Sodium: 836mg;

Classic Coleslaw

Servings:6
Cooking Time: None
Ingredients:

- 1 cup mayonnaise
- 3 tablespoons Dijon mustard
- 1 tablespoon white-wine vinegar
- Juice of 1 lemon
- Pinch sugar
- ½ teaspoon celery seed
- Several dashes onion- and garlic-free hot-pepper sauce
- ¾ teaspoon salt
- ½ teaspoon freshly ground black pepper
- 1 head green cabbage, shredded
- 2 carrots, grated
- 1 fresh red chile, sliced

Directions:

1. In a large bowl, combine the mayonnaise, mustard, vinegar, lemon juice, sugar, celery seed, hot sauce, salt, and pepper, and stir together.
2. Add the cabbage and carrots to the dressing, and toss together until evenly coated.
3. Cover and chill the coleslaw for at least 2 hours before serving.

Nutrition Info:

- InfoCalories: 198; Protein: 5g; Total Fat: 14g; Saturated Fat: 2g; Carbohydrates: 19g; Fiber: 4g; Sodium: 694mg;

Curried Potato And Parsnip Soup

Servings:4
Cooking Time:x
Ingredients:

- 1 tablespoon canola oil
- 2 parsnips (14 ounces/400 g), peeled and cut into ¾-inch (2 cm) pieces
- 4 potatoes (1¾ pounds/800 g), peeled and cut into ¾-inch (2 cm) pieces
- 6½ cups (1.5 liters) gluten-free, onion-free chicken or vegetable stock*
- 1 teaspoon gluten-free curry powder, or to taste
- 1 cup (250 ml) low-fat milk, lactose-free milk, or suitable plant-based milk
- Salt and freshly ground black pepper
- Chopped flat-leaf parsley, to garnish

Directions:

1. Heat the canola oil in a large heavy-bottomed saucepan over medium heat. Add the parsnips and potatoes and cook, stirring regularly, for 3 to 5 minutes, until lightly golden. Add the stock and bring to a boil. Reduce the heat and simmer for 15 to 20 minutes, stirring occasionally, until the vegetables are tender. Remove from the heat and let cool for about 10 minutes.
2. Puree with an immersion blender (or in batches in a regular blender) until smooth. Add the curry powder and milk and blend again until well combined. Season to taste with salt and pepper. Reheat gently without boiling. Garnish with a sprinkling of parsley and serve.

Nutrition Info:

- Info: 215 calories,10 g protein,4 g total fat,36 g carbohydrates,766 mg sodiu.

Potato Soup

Servings:4
Cooking Time:x
Ingredients:

- 6 medium russet potatoes, peeled and cut into cubes
- ¼ cup butter
- ½ cup gluten-free all-purpose flour
- 6 cups lactose-free milk
- ⅛ teaspoon salt
- ¼ teaspoon cracked black pepper
- ¼ pound grated Cheddar cheese
- ¼ pound grated Parmesan cheese
- 1 green onion, green part only, diced

Directions:

1. Boil potatoes in a large pot until tender, about 15 minutes. Drain and add potatoes to a food processor; blend until smooth.
2. In a large saucepan, melt butter over medium heat. Add flour and cook about 1 minute, stirring continuously.
3. Add 3 cups milk to pan with salt and pepper; stir until there are no lumps. Add potatoes and remaining milk and increase heat to medium-high; bring to a rolling boil, stirring constantly.
4. After boiling, turn heat off and add cheese and green onion. Stir until cheese is melted. Serve immediately in soup bowls.

Nutrition Info:

- InfoCalories: 504,Fat: 21g,Protein: 24g,Sodium: 733mg,Carbohydrates: 54.

Pumpkin Cornbread

Servings: 8
Cooking Time:25 Minutes
Ingredients:

- 1 ¼ cups corn flour
- 1 cup gluten-free, all-purpose flour
- 2 tsp of baking powder
- ¾ tsp of baking soda
- 1 tbsp white sugar
- 1 tbsp brown sugar
- Pinch of salt
- 1 ½ tsp sage, dried
- ½ cup spring onions, green part only
- 1 cup cheese, cheddar or any other approved
- 1 cup pumpkin, puréed
- 1 cup lactose-free milk
- 2 tbsp olive oil

Directions:
1. Preheat the oven to 350°F.
2. Chop the spring onions finely and grate the cheese.
3. Mix the flour, baking powder, baking soda, sugar, salt, and sage together in a bowl.
4. Melt the butter and use it to grease an ovenproof skillet. Once greased, add the remainder of the butter in the bowl.
5. Mix all the ingredients together thoroughly, then scoop and spread the mixture into the skillet.
6. Bake for 30-35 minutes. When finished, the top should be golden. Insert a skewer into the middle of the pan, and if it comes out clean, the bread is fully cooked.

Nutrition Info:
- Info230g Cal,5.8 g Fat ,39.5 g Carbs ,4.9 g Protein.

Abundantly Happy Kale Salad

Servings:5
Cooking Time:x
Ingredients:

- 9 large leaves curly kale, thinly shredded (ribs and stems removed)
- 1⁄2 teaspoon sea salt
- 3 tablespoons extra-virgin olive oil, divided
- Juice of 1 large lemon
- 1 cup shredded butter lettuce
- 1 medium stalk celery, diced
- 1 medium yellow bell pepper, seeded and diced
- 1 medium carrot, peeled and grated
- 1 tablespoon hemp seeds
- 1 tablespoon pumpkin seeds
- 1 tablespoon chopped walnuts
- 2 cups shredded common (green) cabbage
- 2 radishes, sliced very thin
- 1 cup sliced fennel bulb
- 1 cup fresh blueberries

Directions:

1. Add kale to a medium bowl and sprinkle salt and 2 tablespoons oil on top. Massage leaves with hands until leaves begin to darken and soften.
2. Add remaining oil and remaining ingredients and toss gently. Keep covered in refrigerator up to 3 days.

Nutrition Info:
- InfoCalories: 163,Fat: 11g,Protein: 4g,Sodium: 289mg,Carbohydrates: 17.

Shrimp Bisque

Servings:6
Cooking Time:x
Ingredients:

- 1 tablespoon extra-virgin olive oil
- 4 medium carrots, peeled and sliced into 1⁄4" rounds
- 1 medium red bell pepper, seeded and diced
- 4 cups Basic Roast Chicken Stock (see recipe in this chapter)
- 1 (14.5-ounce) can diced tomatoes
- 11⁄2 pounds uncooked shrimp, peeled and deveined
- 1⁄2 cup lactose-free milk
- 1⁄4 cup white wine
- 1 pinch crushed red pepper
- 2 tablespoons chopped fresh flat-leaf parsley

Directions:

1. Heat olive oil in a stockpot over medium-high heat. Add carrots and red bell pepper and sauté for 5 minutes.
2. Add stock and tomatoes. Bring to a boil, then lower heat and simmer, uncovered, for 15 minutes.
3. As soup is simmering, divide shrimp into 2 piles and set 1 pile aside. Take the remaining shrimp and cut each into thirds.
4. Once the soup has simmered for 15 minutes, add the whole shrimp to the pot. Cook for 5 minutes until shrimp is cooked through.
5. Pour contents of stockpot into a blender, working in batches if necessary. Blend until smooth.
6. Return soup to pot. Add milk, wine, and crushed red pepper. Simmer uncovered for 2 minutes.
7. Add chopped shrimp to pot and cook through, 5 minutes. Serve soup with a garnish of parsley.

Nutrition Info:

- InfoCalories: 175,Fat: 7g,Protein: 30g,Sodium: 405mg,Carbohydrates: 11.

Easy Rice Pilaf

Servings:4
Cooking Time:10 Minutes
Ingredients:

- 2 tablespoons extra-virgin olive oil
- 6 scallions, green parts only, chopped
- 2 carrots, chopped
- 2 cups cooked brown rice
- 1⁄4 cup pine nuts
- 1⁄2 teaspoon sea salt
- 1⁄8 teaspoon freshly ground black pepper
- 1⁄4 cup chopped fresh parsley leaves

Directions:

1. In a large skillet over medium-high heat, heat the olive oil until it shimmers.
2. Add the scallions and carrots. Cook for about 4 minutes, stirring occasionally.
3. Stir in the brown rice, pine nuts, salt, and pepper. Cook for about 5 minutes more, stirring occasionally, until the rice is warm.
4. Stir in the parsley just before serving.

Nutrition Info:

- InfoCalories: 307,Total Fat: 13g,Carbohydrates: 43g,Sodium: 263mg,Protein: 5.

Sauces, Dressings, And Condiments Recipes

Bolognese Sauce

Servings:8
Cooking Time:x
Ingredients:

- 2 tablespoons extra-virgin olive oil
- 2 tablespoons butter
- 1 medium yellow onion, peeled and quartered
- 2 garlic cloves, peeled, slightly smashed
- 1 1/2 cups finely diced carrots
- 1 pound ground meatball mix (beef, pork, and veal)
- 1/2 cup dry white wine
- 1 teaspoon sea salt
- 1/8 teaspoon freshly ground black pepper
- 1/8 teaspoon ground nutmeg
- 1 (14.5-ounce) can diced fire-roasted tomatoes
- 1 tablespoon Tomato Paste (see recipe in this chapter)
- 1 (1" × 3") Parmesan cheese rind
- 1/2 cup Whipped Cream (see recipe in Chapter 14)

Directions:

1. Heat oil and butter over medium-low heat in a large stockpot. Add the onion and garlic and sauté, stirring constantly, until garlic is softened and brown at edges. Remove and discard onion and garlic, leaving oil and butter.
2. Add carrots to oil and sauté over medium-low heat for 15 minutes, stirring occasionally.
3. Add meat and cook, stirring often to break up into bits, for about 10–15 minutes or until meat is fully browned.
4. Add wine and simmer uncovered 10 minutes.
5. Add salt, pepper, nutmeg, tomatoes, paste, and rind, and simmer uncovered 1 1/2–2 hours more, stirring occasionally.
6. Remove rind, fold in whipped cream, and serve.

Nutrition Info:

- InfoCalories: 210,Fat: 14g,Protein: 12g,Sodium: 415mg,Carbohydrates: 6.

Low-fodmap Vegetable Broth

Servings:8
Cooking Time: 3 To 8 Hours
Ingredients:

- 3 carrots, roughly chopped
- 2 leeks, green parts only, roughly chopped
- 1 fennel bulb, roughly chopped
- 8 peppercorns
- 1 fresh rosemary sprig

Directions:

1. In a large stockpot or slow cooker, combine the carrots, leeks, fennel, peppercorns, and rosemary.
2. Fill the pot about ¾ full, with enough water to cover the ingredients.
3. If using a stockpot: Place the pot over medium-low heat and bring the liquid to a simmer.
4. Simmer for 3 hours.
5. If using a slow cooker: Cover the cooker, set the temperature to low, and cook for 8 hours.
6. Strain and discard the solids. Refrigerate or freeze the stock in 1-cup servings. The broth will keep in the refrigerator for about 5 days or in the freezer for up to 12 months.

Nutrition Info:

- InfoCalories:15; Total Fat: 0g; Saturated Fat: 0g; Carbohydrates: 5g; Fiber: 0g; Sodium: 30mg; Protein: <1g

Garden Pesto

Servings:1
Cooking Time:x
Ingredients:

- 2 tablespoons Garlic-Infused Oil (see recipe in this chapter)
- 1/4 cup pine nuts, toasted
- 1 cup packed basil leaves
- 1/2 teaspoon sea salt
- 1/4 cup freshly grated Parmesan cheese

Directions:

1. Add all ingredients to a food processor and blend to a pesto consistency.

Nutrition Info:

- InfoCalories: 178,Fat: 17g,Protein: 5g,Sodium: 350mg,Carbohydrates: 2.

Traditional Tomato Sauce

Servings:6
Cooking Time:x
Ingredients:

- 1/4 cup extra-virgin olive oil
- 1 medium onion, peeled and quartered
- 4 garlic cloves, peeled and slightly smashed
- 11/2 cups Tomato Purée (see recipe in this chapter)
- 1 (14-ounce) can San Marzano diced tomatoes
- 1 (14-ounce) can whole peeled San Marzano tomatoes
- 1 teaspoon dried oregano
- 1 teaspoon dried basil
- 1 tablespoon turbinado sugar
- 1 (1" × 3") Parmesan cheese rind

Directions:

1. Heat oil over medium-low heat in a large saucepan. Add the onion and garlic and sauté, stirring constantly, until garlic is softened and brown at edges. Remove and discard onion and garlic, leaving oil.
2. Add remaining ingredients, except for cheese rind; stir to combine. Break up whole tomatoes with a pair of kitchen shears.
3. Bring just to a boil, then reduce heat to low. Add cheese rind and simmer uncovered, stirring occasionally, for 11/2–2 hours. Remove remainder of rind before serving.

Nutrition Info:

- InfoCalories: 180,Fat: 12g,Protein: 3g,Sodium: 825mg,Carbohydrates: 19.

Tomato Purée

Servings:11
Cooking Time:x
Ingredients:

- 1 tablespoon Garlic-Infused Oil (see recipe in this chapter)
- 5 medium ripe tomatoes, cored, seeded, and diced
- 1 teaspoon sea salt
- 1/4 teaspoon freshly ground black pepper

Directions:

1. Heat oil over medium-low heat in a large saucepan. Add tomatoes to oil and stir. Season with salt and pepper. Sauté, stirring occasionally, for 15–20 minutes, until tomatoes are soft and broken down. Remove from heat to cool.
2. Transfer cooled tomatoes to a food processor and blend completely. Set a large strainer over a large bowl. Transfer purée to strainer. Press down with a large spoon to completely separate solids in strainer from purée in bowl.
3. Transfer to an airtight container and store in the refrigerator.

Nutrition Info:

- InfoCalories: 77,Fat: 5g,Protein: 2g,Sodium: 795mg,Carbohydrates: 8.

Thai Sweet Chili Sauce

Servings:1
Cooking Time: 7 Minutes
Ingredients:

* 1 cup plus 2 tablespoons water, divided
* 2 tablespoons cornstarch
* 2 tablespoons finely chopped chiles (use red jalapeños, red Thai, Fresno, or other red chiles)
* ⅔ cup sugar
* ⅓ cup rice vinegar
* 2 teaspoons salt

Directions:

1. In a small bowl, stir together 2 tablespoons of the water and the cornstarch until smooth.
2. In a medium saucepan over medium heat, combine the remaining 1 cup water, chiles, sugar, vinegar, and salt, and bring to a boil. Reduce the heat to low and simmer, uncovered, until the sauce starts to become syrupy, about 5 minutes.
3. Give the cornstarch mixture a stir and whisk it into the simmering sauce. Cook, stirring, for 1 minute more, until the sauce is thickened. Remove from the heat and let cool slightly before using.
4. Store in a covered container in the refrigerator for up to a week.

Nutrition Info:

* InfoCalories: 85; Protein: 0g; Total Fat: 0g; Saturated Fat: 0g; Carbohydrates: 20g; Fiber: 0g; Sodium: 582mg;

Pork Loin Rub

Servings:1
Cooking Time:x
Ingredients:

* 1 tablespoon sea salt
* 1 tablespoon demerara sugar
* 1 tablespoon ground cinnamon
* 1 tablespoon sweet paprika
* 1 teaspoon dried oregano
* 1/2 teaspoon ground cumin
* 1/2 teaspoon ground red pepper

Directions:

1. Mix all ingredients together in a small bowl.

Nutrition Info:

* InfoCalories: 19,Fat: 0g,Protein: 0g,Sodium: 1,410mg,Carbohydrates: 5.

Tahini Dressing

Servings:3
Cooking Time:x
Ingredients:

* 1/4 cup tahini
* 1/4 cup water
* 2 tablespoons fresh lemon juice
* 1 tablespoon maple syrup
* 1/4 teaspoon pink Himalayan salt
* 1/4 teaspoon freshly ground black pepper

Directions:

1. Combine all ingredients in a blender or food processor. Store in an air-tight container at room temperature for 1–2 weeks.

Nutrition Info:

* InfoCalories: 70,Fat: 5g,Protein: 2g,Sodium: 111mg,Carbohydrates: 5.

Clever Curry Mayonnaise

Servings:1
Cooking Time:x
Ingredients:

- 1 cup Basic Mayonnaise (see recipe in this chapter)
- 2 teaspoons curry powder (without onions or garlic)
- 1/2 tablespoon fresh lime juice
- 1/2 tablespoon fresh lemon juice
- 1/8 teaspoon cayenne pepper
- 1/8 teaspoon paprika

Directions:

1. Place all ingredients in a food processor and pulse to a smooth consistency. If storing, place in a container with a tight-fitting lid in refrigerator up to 3 days.

Nutrition Info:

- InfoCalories: 100,Fat: 11g,Protein: 0g,Sodium: 79mg,Carbohydrates: 1.

Basil "hollandaise" Sauce

Servings:1
Cooking Time: None
Ingredients:

- ½ cup cold rice milk
- ½ cup fresh basil leaves
- 4 teaspoons lemon juice
- 1 tablespoon nutritional yeast
- ½ teaspoon salt
- ⅛ teaspoon cayenne pepper
- ⅛ teaspoon turmeric
- ¼ teaspoon xanthan gum
- ½ cup light olive oil

Directions:

1. In a blender, combine the rice milk, basil, lemon juice, nutritional yeast, salt, cayenne, and turmeric, and process until smooth.
2. Add the xanthan gum and blend on high until the mixture becomes foamy.
3. With the blender running, slowly add the oil, blending until the sauce is thick.

Nutrition Info:

- InfoCalories: 161; Protein: 1g; Total Fat: 17g; Saturated Fat: 2g; Carbohydrates: 3g; Fiber: 0g; Sodium: 203mg;

Strawberry Chia Seed Jam

Servings:1
Cooking Time:x
Ingredients:

- 1/2 pint (or 6 ounces) fresh strawberries
- 1 tablespoon lemon juice
- 2 1/2 tablespoons pure maple syrup
- 1 tablespoon chia seeds

Directions:

1. Add fruit, lemon juice, and maple syrup to a small saucepan and cook over medium-high heat. Cover. Stir occasionally until fruit begins to thicken, about 10 minutes.
2. Uncover and bring mixture to a boil until it develops a sauce-like consistency, about 5 minutes.
3. Stir in chia seeds and cook 2 more minutes. Stir again and then remove from heat.
4. Transfer jam to an airtight jar or other container and allow to cool, or refrigerate 2–3 hours before use. The jam will continue to thicken. Can be stored in refrigerator 2 weeks or frozen up to 2 months.

Nutrition Info:

- InfoCalories: 26,Fat: 0g,Protein: 0g,Sodium: 2mg,Carbohydrates: 6.

Blueberry Chia Seed Jam

Servings:1
Cooking Time:x
Ingredients:
- ½ pint (or 6 ounces) fresh blueberries
- 1 tablespoon lemon juice
- 2½ tablespoons pure maple syrup
- 1 tablespoon chia seeds

Directions:
1. Add fruit, lemon juice, and maple syrup to a small saucepan and cook over medium-high heat. Cover. Stir occasionally until fruit begins to thicken, about 10 minutes.
2. Uncover and bring mixture to a boil until it develops a sauce-like consistency, about 5 minutes.
3. Stir in chia seeds and cook 2 more minutes. Stir again and then remove from heat.
4. Transfer jam to an airtight jar or other container and allow to cool, or refrigerate 2–3 hours before use. The jam will continue to thicken. Can be stored in refrigerator 2 weeks or frozen up to 2 months.

Nutrition Info:
- InfoCalories: 34,Fat: 1g,Protein: 0g,Sodium: 1mg,Carbohydrates: 7.

Dill Dipping Sauce

Servings:3
Cooking Time:x
Ingredients:
- 3 tablespoons chopped fresh dill
- 1 tablespoon lemon juice
- 7 ounces lactose-free sour cream
- ¼ teaspoon salt

Directions:
1. In a food processor combine all ingredients and process until smooth. Use immediately or transfer to an airtight container and store in refrigerator for 3–4 days.

Nutrition Info:
- InfoCalories: 64,Fat: 7g,Protein: 1g,Sodium: 125mg,Carbohydrates: 1.

Egg-free Caesar Dressing

Servings:1
Cooking Time: None
Ingredients:
- 4 whole anchovy fillets
- 2 tablespoons Dijon mustard
- 1 tablespoon red-wine vinegar
- 1 teaspoon gluten-free soy sauce or coconut aminos
- Juice of ½ lemon
- ¼ teaspoon salt
- ¼ teaspoon freshly ground black pepper
- ¼ cup olive oil
- ¼ cup Garlic Oil (here)
- ¼ cup freshly grated Parmesan cheese

Directions:
1. In a blender or food processor, combine the anchovies, mustard, vinegar, soy sauce or coconut aminos, lemon juice, salt, and pepper. Pulse to chop the anchovies and combine well.
2. With the processor running, slowly add the olive oil and Garlic Oil in a thin stream. Process until the mixture is thickened. Add the cheese and pulse just to incorporate.
3. Serve immediately or store in a covered container in the refrigerator for up to a week.

Nutrition Info:
- InfoCalories: 229; Protein: 18g; Total Fat: 17g; Saturated Fat: 4g; Carbohydrates: 2g; Fiber: 0g; Sodium: 3632mg;

Chimichurri Sauce

Servings:1
Cooking Time: None
Ingredients:

- 1 cup fresh flat-leaf parsley
- ¼ cup lemon juice
- ¼ cup olive oil
- ¼ cup Garlic Oil (here)
- ¼ cup fresh cilantro
- ¾ teaspoon red-pepper flakes
- ½ teaspoon ground cumin
- ½ teaspoon salt

Directions:

1. Combine all the ingredients in a blender or food processor and process until smooth.
2. Use immediately or cover and refrigerate for up to a week.

Nutrition Info:

- InfoCalories: 88; Protein: 1g; Total Fat: 9g; Saturated Fat: 1g; Carbohydrates: 3g; Fiber: 1g; Sodium: 203mg;

Raspberry Sauce

Servings:4
Cooking Time: 10 Minutes
Ingredients:

- 1 cup fresh raspberries
- ¼ cup sugar
- 2 tablespoons water

Directions:

1. In a large saucepan over medium-high heat, cook the raspberries, sugar, and water, stirring frequently and mashing the raspberries with a spoon. Bring to a boil. Reduce the heat to low and simmer for 5 minutes.
2. Strain the sauce through a fine-mesh sieve to remove the seeds. Chill before serving.

Nutrition Info:

- InfoCalories:63; Total Fat: 0g; Saturated Fat: 0g; Carbohydrates: 16g; Fiber: 2g; Sodium: 1mg; Protein: <1g

Luscious Hot Fudge Sauce

Servings:2
Cooking Time: 5 Minutes
Ingredients:

- ⅔ cup full-fat coconut milk
- ½ cup granulated sugar
- ⅓ cup brown sugar
- ¼ cup unsweetened cocoa powder
- ¼ teaspoon salt
- 6 ounces bittersweet chocolate (dairy-free and gluten-free), chopped, divided
- 2 tablespoons coconut oil
- 1 teaspoon vanilla extract

Directions:

1. In a medium saucepan combine the coconut milk, sugars, cocoa powder, salt, and half of the chocolate, and bring to a boil. Reduce the heat to low and simmer, stirring occasionally, for 5 minutes.
2. Remove the pan from the heat and whisk in the remaining chocolate along with the coconut oil and vanilla. Stir until smooth.
3. Let cool for 15 to 20 minutes before serving. Serve warm or store in a covered container in the refrigerator for up to 2 weeks.

Nutrition Info:

- InfoCalories: 135; Protein: 2g; Total Fat: 8g; Saturated Fat: 6g; Carbohydrates: 17g; Fiber: 1g; Sodium: 48mg;

Italian Vegetable Sauce

Servings:6
Cooking Time:x
Ingredients:

- 2 tablespoons extra-virgin olive oil
- 2 medium red bell peppers, seeded and diced
- 2 medium green bell peppers, seeded and diced
- 4 large carrots, peeled and cut into thin rounds
- 2 medium zucchini, quartered lengthwise and cut into 1/4" slices
- 1 (28-ounce) can whole tomatoes
- 2 tablespoons demerara sugar
- 1 tablespoon dried basil
- 1 tablespoon dried oregano
- 1/2 teaspoon ground cinnamon
- 1/2 teaspoon ground dried ginger
- 1 pinch crushed red pepper
- 1/8 teaspoon sea salt
- 1/8 teaspoon freshly ground black pepper

Directions:

1. Heat olive oil in a large stockpot over medium-high heat. Add bell peppers, carrots, and zucchini to pot and sauté until crisp-tender, approximately 10 minutes, stirring frequently.
2. Add tomatoes (breaking them up with your hands), sugar, basil, oregano, cinnamon, ginger, crushed red pepper, salt, and black pepper. Bring to a boil, then simmer, uncovered, for 60 minutes.

Nutrition Info:

- InfoCalories: 130,Fat: 5g,Protein: 3g,Sodium: 275mg,Carbohydrates: 21.

Sun-dried Tomato Spread

Servings:x
Cooking Time:x
Ingredients:

- 1 cup (150 g) sun-dried tomatoes in oil, drained and roughly chopped (oil reserved)
- 1/4 cup (15 g) roughly chopped flat-leaf parsley
- 2 heaping tablespoons reduced-fat cream cheese, at room temperature
- 1 tablespoon garlic-infused olive oil
- 3 tablespoons olive oil
- Salt and freshly ground black pepper

Directions:

1. Place the sun-dried tomatoes and reserved oil, parsley, and cream cheese in a food processor or blender and process until well combined.
2. Gradually add the garlic-infused oil and olive oil until the mixture is almost smooth.
3. Season to taste with salt and pepper.
4. Spoon into a bowl or jar, cover, and store in the fridge for up to 3 days.

Nutrition Info:

- Info134 calories; 1 g protein; 13 g total fat; 3 g saturated fat; 3 g carbohydrates; 1 g fiber; 122 mg sodium

Sweet Barbecue Sauce

Servings:1
Cooking Time:x
Ingredients:

- 1 cup Tomato Purée (see recipe in this chapter)
- 1 tablespoon Dijon mustard
- 1 tablespoon blackstrap molasses
- 1 1/2 tablespoons pure maple syrup
- 1/2 teaspoon ground cinnamon
- 1/2 teaspoon ground cumin
- 1/2 teaspoon dried oregano
- 1/2 teaspoon white wine vinegar
- 1/2 teaspoon arrowroot powder
- 1/2 teaspoon paprika
- 1/8 teaspoon ground red pepper
- 1/8 teaspoon nutmeg
- 1/8 teaspoon sea salt

Directions:

1. Bring all ingredients just to a boil in a small saucepan over medium-high heat. Lower heat and simmer, uncovered, 5–10 minutes, or until sauce thickens.

Nutrition Info:

- InfoCalories: 25,Fat: 0g,Protein: 1g,Sodium: 100mg,Carbohydrates: 6.

Basil Sauce

Servings:1
Cooking Time:x
Ingredients:

- 1/4 cup tahini
- 1/4 cup fresh flat-leaf parsley leaves
- 1/4 cup coarsely chopped fresh chives
- 1 packed cup fresh basil
- Juice of 2 medium lemons
- 1/4 cup olive oil
- 1/4 teaspoon sea salt
- 1/4 teaspoon freshly ground black pepper

Directions:

1. Add all ingredients to a food processor. Blend until smooth. Store in an air-tight container in refrigerator for 5–7 days or in freezer for 3–4 months.

Nutrition Info:

- InfoCalories: 56,Fat: 5g,Protein: 1g,Sodium: 42mg,Carbohydrates: 2.

Pesto Sauce

Servings:11
Cooking Time:x
Ingredients:

- 3/4 packed cup fresh basil leaves
- 1/8 cup garlic-infused olive oil
- 1/4 cup pine nuts
- 1/8 cup extra-virgin olive oil
- 1/2 cup freshly grated Parmesan cheese
- 1/8 teaspoon sea salt
- 1/8 teaspoon freshly ground black pepper

Directions:

1. Combine basil, garlic oil, and pine nuts in a food processor and pulse until coarsely chopped.
2. Add extra-virgin olive oil, cheese, salt, and pepper and process until fully incorporated and smooth. Use immediately or transfer to an airtight container and store in refrigerator for 4–5 days or in freezer for 1–2 months.

Nutrition Info:

- InfoCalories: 142,Fat: 13g,Protein: 5g,Sodium: 237mg,Carbohydrates: 2.

Basil Pesto

Servings:x
Cooking Time:x

Ingredients:
- 2 handfuls of basil leaves, rinsed and dried
- 2 tablespoons garlic-infused olive oil
- 2 tablespoons olive oil, plus more as needed
- ⅓ cup (50 g) pine nuts
- ⅓ cup (25 g) grated Parmesan
- Salt and freshly ground black pepper

Directions:
1. Combine the basil, garlic-infused oil, olive oil, pine nuts, and Parmesan in a food processor or blender and process until well combined.
2. Season to taste with salt and pepper.
3. Add more oil if you prefer a more liquid pesto for drizzling.
4. Spoon into a bowl or jar and cover with a thin layer of olive oil.
5. Cover and store in the fridge for up to 5 days or in the freezer for up to 2 months.

Nutrition Info:
- Info107 calories; 3 g protein; 10 g total fat; 2 g saturated fat; 1 g carbohydrates; 0 g fiber; 102 mg sodium

Maple Mustard Dipping Sauce

Servings:4
Cooking Time:x

Ingredients:
- 1 tablespoon light sour cream
- 1 tablespoon pure maple syrup
- 1 tablespoon Dijon mustard

Directions:
1. Whisk together all ingredients in a small bowl and serve.

Nutrition Info:
- InfoCalories: 20,Fat: 0g,Protein: 0g,Sodium: 45mg,Carbohydrates: 4.

Low-fodmap Mayonnaise

Servings:1
Cooking Time: 0 Minutes

Ingredients:
- 1 egg yolk
- 1 tablespoon red wine vinegar
- ½ teaspoon Dijon mustard
- ¼ teaspoon sea salt
- ¾ cup extra-virgin olive oil

Directions:
1. In a blender or food processor, combine the egg yolk, vinegar, mustard, and salt. Process for about 30 seconds until well combined. With a rubber spatula, scrape down the sides of the blender jar or food processor bowl.
2. Turn the blender or processor to medium speed. Very slowly, drip in the olive oil, 1 drop at a time as the processor or blender runs. After about 10 drops, leave the blender or processor running, then add the rest of the olive oil in a thin stream until it is incorporated and emulsified.
3. The mayo will keep refrigerated for up to 5 days.

Nutrition Info:
- InfoCalories:169; Total Fat: 20g; Saturated Fat: 3g; Carbohydrates: <1g; Fiber: 0g; Sodium: 63mg; Protein: <1g

Snacks & Desserts Recipes

Pineapple, Yogurt On Rice Cakes

Servings:1
Cooking Time: 12 Minutes
Ingredients:

- 2 rice cakes
- ⅓ cup fresh pineapple, sliced
- 2 tbsp Greek yogurt
- ¼ tsp chia seeds, optional
- 1 tsp oil, used to prevent the pineapple from burning

Directions:

1. Spray the pineapple slices with oil, then place them on a tray in the oven and bake for 5 minutes on each side. Cut into chunky pieces.
2. Spread the yogurt over the rice cake and top with pineapple and chia seeds.

Nutrition Info:

- Info169g Calories, 1.5g Total fat, 0.4g Saturated fat, 35.6g Carbohydrates, 1.5 g Fiber, 3.8g Protein, 10g Sodium.

Chocolate Soufflés

Servings:6
Cooking Time:x
Ingredients:

- Nonstick cooking spray
- 1¼ cups (275 g) superfine sugar
- 8 ounces (225 g) good-quality dark chocolate, broken into pieces
- ½ cup (125 ml) light cream
- 6 large eggs, separated
- ⅔ cup (100 g) cornstarch
- ¼ cup (55 g) packed light brown sugar
- ½ cup (125 ml) low-fat milk, lactose-free milk, or suitable plant-based milk
- Confectioners' sugar, sifted (optional)

Directions:

1. Preheat the oven to 350°F (180°C).
2. Grease six 8-ounce (250 ml) soufflé dishes with cooking spray. Place 1 tablespoon of the superfine sugar in each dish and turn to coat generously, discarding any excess.
3. Combine the chocolate and cream in a heatproof bowl or the top part of a double boiler. Set over a saucepan of simmering water or the bottom part of the double boiler (make sure the bottom of the bowl does not touch the water) and stir until the chocolate is melted and well combined. Set aside to cool slightly.
4. Combine the egg yolks and remaining superfine sugar in a large bowl and beat with a handheld electric mixer until pale, thick, and creamy. Gradually beat in the cornstarch, brown sugar, and milk until combined. Pour into a saucepan and cook, stirring, over medium heat for 5 minutes, or until thickened. Stir into the chocolate mixture and set aside to cool slightly.
5. Clean the mixer beaters and beat the egg whites in a large clean bowl until stiff peaks form. Gently fold into the chocolate mixture with a large metal spoon, Fill the soufflé dishes to approximately ¼ inch (5 mm) below the rim.
6. Place the dishes on a baking sheet and bake for 20 to 25 minutes, until the soufflés are nicely risen. Dust with confectioners' sugar, if desired, and serve immediately, as they will sink if left standing.

Nutrition Info:

- Info544 calories; 10 g protein; 22 g total fat; 12 g saturated fat; 85 g carbohydrates; 3 g fiber; 89 mg sodium

Low-fodmap Hummus

Servings:4
Cooking Time: 0 Minutes
Ingredients:

- 1 zucchini
- 2 tablespoons tahini
- 2 tablespoons Garlic Oil
- Juice of 1 lemon
- ½ teaspoon sea salt
- Assorted low-FODMAP veggies, for dipping

Directions:

1. In a blender, combine the zucchini, tahini, garlic oil, lemon juice, and salt. Process until smooth.
2. Serve with the veggies for dipping.

Nutrition Info:

- InfoCalories:116; Total Fat: 11g; Saturated Fat: 2g; Carbohydrates: 4g; Fiber: 1g; Sodium: 251mg; Protein: 2g

Pineapple Salsa

Servings:2
Cooking Time: None
Ingredients:

- 2 cups chopped pineapple
- 2 jalapeño chiles, seeded and finely chopped
- ¼ cup finely chopped cilantro
- ½ teaspoon salt
- Juice of 1 lime
- 1 tablespoon olive oil

Directions:

1. In a medium bowl, stir all of the ingredients together until well combined.
2. Let sit at room temperature for 15 to 20 minutes before serving to allow the flavors to blend.

Nutrition Info:

- InfoCalories: 73; Protein: 1g; Total Fat: 4g; Saturated Fat: 1g; Carbohydrates: 11g; Fiber: 1g; Sodium: 292mg;

Prosciutto-wrapped Cantaloupe

Servings:4
Cooking Time: 0 Minutes
Ingredients:

- 8 (½- to 1-inch-thick) cantaloupe wedges, rind removed
- 8 thin prosciutto slices

Directions:

1. Wrap each melon wedge in a slice of prosciutto and secure it with a toothpick.
2. Chill or serve immediately.

Nutrition Info:

- InfoCalories:73; Total Fat: 2g; Saturated Fat: <1g; Carbohydrates: 4g; Fiber: 0g; Sodium: 517mg; Protein: 9g

Lemon Bar

Servings:16
Cooking Time: 50 Minutes
Ingredients:

- Crust
- 1 ½ cups gluten-free flour
- ½ cup white sugar
- ½ cup butter, unsalted
- 2 tbsp water
- Lemon
- 4 eggs, large
- ½ cup lemon juice
- 1 ½ cups sugar
- ¼ cup gluten-free flour
- Powdered sugar, to dust on top

Directions:

1. Preheat the oven to 350°F. Grease a square baking pan (9.5 inches by 9.5 inches) with butter and set aside.
2. Mix the flour and sugar together. Mix the butter into the flour until the mixture reaches a crumbly consistency. Add the water and mix well. Press into the bottom of the pan and bake for 20-25 minutes.
3. In another bowl, whisk the eggs, lemon juice, sugar, and flour until smooth. Pour onto the baked crust.
4. Bake for another 25 minutes, remove from the oven, and allow to cool.

Nutrition Info:

- Info212g Calories, 7.3g Total fat, 5.2g Saturated fat, 35.1g Carbohydrates, 1.4 g Fiber, 3.4g Protein, 25g Sodium.

Almond Cookies

Servings:x
Cooking Time:x
Ingredients:

- MAKES ABOUT 40
- ¾ cup (90 g) almond flour
- 1 tablespoon plus 1 teaspoon cornstarch
- ½ teaspoon gluten-free baking powder
- 1 large egg white
- ½ cup (110 g) superfine sugar
- 1 teaspoon finely grated lemon zest
- 3 drops almond extract
- 1 tablespoon (15 g) unsalted butter, melted

Directions:

1. Preheat the oven to 275°F (140°C). Line two baking sheets with parchment paper.
2. Combine the almond flour, cornstarch, and baking powder in a small bowl. Beat the egg white in a clean medium bowl with a handheld electric mixer until soft peaks form. Gradually beat in the sugar. Continue beating for 5 minutes more or until stiff peaks form. Add the almond flour mixture, lemon zest, almond extract, and melted butter and gently mix together with a large metal spoon.
3. Roll 2 teaspoons of the dough into a ball. Repeat with the remaining dough to make about 40 balls, placing them on the baking sheets and leaving a little room for spreading. Flatten slightly. Bake for 25 minutes, until they have started turning a light golden brown.
4. Cool on the sheets for 5 minutes, then transfer to a wire rack to cool completely.

Nutrition Info:

- Info25 calories; 1 g protein; 1 g total fat; 0 g saturated fat; 3 g carbohydrates; 0 g fiber; 7 mg sodium

Hazelnut Or Almond Crescents

Servings:x
Cooking Time:x
Ingredients:

- MAKES ABOUT 40
- ⅓ cup (45 g) superfine white rice flour, plus more for the work surface
- ¼ cup (35 g) cornstarch
- ¼ cup (55 g) superfine sugar
- 1¼ cups (125 g) hazelnut or almond flour
- 7 tablespoons (105 g) unsalted butter, cut into cubes, at room temperature
- 1 large egg yolk, at room temperature, lightly beaten
- 1 teaspoon vanilla extract
- ½ cup (80 g) confectioners' sugar, plus more for dusting

Directions:

1. Sift the rice flour and cornstarch into a medium bowl (or whisk in the bowl until well combined). Stir in the superfine sugar and hazelnut flour. Rub in the butter with your fingertips until the mixture resembles bread crumbs. Mix in the egg yolk and vanilla with a large metal spoon.
2. Lightly sprinkle your work surface with rice flour. Gently press the dough into a ball, turn out onto the floured surface, and knead lightly until smooth. Divide the dough into two even portions, wrap each in plastic wrap, and refrigerate for 15 minutes.
3. While the dough is chilling, preheat the oven to 325°F (160°C). Line two baking sheets with parchment paper.
4. Unwrap the dough and roll each portion into a log with a diameter of about ¾ inch (2 cm). Cut ¾- to 1-inch (2 to 3 cm) slices and shape them into rounded crescents with your hands. Place on the baking sheets, leaving room for spreading.
5. Bake for 15 to 20 minutes, until lightly golden. Let cool on the sheets for 5 minutes.
6. Sift the confectioners' sugar into a shallow bowl (or whisk well in the bowl). Roll the warm cookies in the sugar until well coated, then transfer to a wire rack to cool completely. Dust with extra confectioners' sugar just before serving.

Nutrition Info:

- Info60 calories; 1 g protein; 4 g total fat; 1 g saturated fat; 5 g carbohydrates; 0 g fiber; 0 mg sodium

Chocolate Peanut Butter Cups

Servings:8
Cooking Time: None
Ingredients:

- 1 cup all-natural creamy peanut butter
- 2 tablespoons coconut oil
- 2 tablespoons maple syrup
- Pinch salt
- 1 cup gluten-free, dairy-free, dark chocolate chips

Directions:

1. In a food processor, combine the peanut butter, coconut oil, maple syrup, and salt, and process until smooth and well combined. Spoon the mixture into cups of a mini muffin tin, dividing equally.
2. In the top of a double boiler set over simmering water, or in a microwave, melt the chocolate chips. Pour the melted chocolate over the peanut butter mixture in the muffin cups. Freeze for at least 30 minutes.
3. Pop the cups out of the muffin tin, using the tip of a sharp knife. Keep frozen until serving time, letting the cups sit at room temperature for 5 minutes before serving.

Nutrition Info:

- InfoCalories: 312; Protein: 10g; Total Fat: 23g; Saturated Fat: 8g; Carbohydrates: 19g; Fiber: 2g; Sodium: 140mg;

Caramel Nut Bars

Servings:18
Cooking Time:x
Ingredients:

- Nonstick cooking spray
- ½ cup (65 g) superfine white rice flour
- ¼ cup (45 g) potato flour
- ⅓ cup (50 g) cornstarch
- ¼ cup (55 g) superfine sugar
- ¼ teaspoon baking soda
- ¼ teaspoon gluten-free baking powder
- 1 teaspoon xanthan gum or guar gum
- 4 tablespoons (½ stick/60 g) unsalted butter, cut into cubes, at room temperature
- 1 large egg, beaten
- 1 teaspoon vanilla extract
- 1 cup (220 g) packed light brown sugar
- 10 tablespoons (1 stick plus 2 tablespoons/150 g) unsalted butter, cut into cubes, at room temperature
- ⅓ cup (80 ml) light cream
- 3 tablespoons plus 1 teaspoon cornstarch
- ½ cup (65 g) roasted unsalted pecans, roughly chopped
- ⅔ cup (110 g) roasted unsalted Brazil nuts (skin on), roughly chopped
- ½ cup (70 g) roasted unsalted macadamia nuts, halved

Directions:

1. Preheat the oven to 350°F (180°C). Grease an 11 x 7-inch (28 x 18 cm) baking pan with cooking spray and line with parchment paper, leaving an overhang on the two long sides to help lift out the bars later.
2. Sift the rice flour, potato flour, cornstarch, superfine sugar, baking soda, baking powder, and xanthan gum together three times into a bowl (or whisk in the bowl until well combined). Rub in the butter with your fingertips. Add the egg and vanilla and mix with a large metal spoon until well combined. As the mixture becomes more solid, use your hands to bring it together to form a ball.
3. Roll out the dough between two sheets of parchment paper to a thickness of ¼ inch (5 mm). Gently fit into the bottom of the pan and prick all over with a fork. Refrigerate for 10 minutes.
4. Bake for 10 to 12 minutes, until the crust is firm and lightly golden. Set aside to cool, but leave the oven on.
5. To make the topping, combine the brown sugar and butter in a large saucepan over medium heat and stir until the butter has melted and the mixture comes to a boil. Remove from the heat and stir in the cream and cornstarch, mixing until smooth. Add the pecans, Brazil nuts, and macadamia nuts. Return the pan to medium heat and stir until the mixture comes to a boil. Reduce the heat to low and cook gently for 2 to 3 minutes more, until the mixture is thick and sticky.
6. Spread the nut topping evenly over the crust and bake for 15 minutes, or until the topping is bubbling. Let cool completely in the pan, then transfer to a board, remove the parchment paper, and cut into small (or large!) pieces to serve.

Nutrition Info:

- Info278 calories; 3 g protein; 20 g total fat; 8 g saturated fat; 25 g carbohydrates; 1 g fiber; 39 mg sodium

Chocolate Fudge Sauce

Servings:16
Cooking Time: 20 Minutes
Ingredients:

- ⅔ cup coconut cream, canned
- 1 cup coconut milk, can substitute with other approved milk
- ¾ cup brown sugar
- 4 tbsp cocoa powder
- 3 tbsp coconut oil
- 1 tsp vanilla extract

Directions:

1. In a blender, mix the ingredients until smooth.
2. Transfer to a small saucepan over medium heat. Bring to a gentle boil for 20 minutes, stirring occasionally to stop the boiling and to mix in any skin that forms.
3. Place in the fridge to cool for 20 minutes. A thin skin will form; whisk it into the sauce. Overnight, the mixture will turn to a fudge-like consistency.

Nutrition Info:

- Info95g Calories, 5.4g Total fat, 4.4g Saturated fat, 12.3g Carbohydrates, 0.7 g Fiber, 0.6g Protein, 10.4g Sodium.

Banana Friands (mini Almond Cakes)

Servings:x
Cooking Time:x
Ingredients:
- MAKES 12
- Nonstick cooking spray
- 9 tablespoons (1 stick plus 1 tablespoon/135 g) unsalted butter, cut into cubes
- 1¼ cups (200 g) confectioners' sugar, plus more for dusting
- ¼ cup (35 g) cornstarch
- ¼ cup (35 g) superfine white rice flour
- 1¼ cups (150 g) almond flour
- 5 large egg whites, lightly beaten
- 1 tablespoon plus 1 teaspoon fresh lemon juice
- 1 teaspoon vanilla extract
- 1 small ripe banana, peeled and roughly chopped

Directions:
1. Preheat the oven to 350°F (180°C). Lightly grease a 12-cup muffin pan, friand pan, or petite loaf pan with cooking spray.
2. Melt the butter in a small saucepan over low heat, then cook for 3 to 4 minutes more, until flecks of brown appear. Set aside.
3. Sift the confectioners' sugar, cornstarch, and rice flour three times into a large bowl (or whisk in the bowl until well combined). Stir in the almond flour, then add the egg whites, lemon juice, vanilla, and melted butter and mix with a large metal spoon until combined. Stir in the chopped banana.
4. Spoon the batter into the pan until each cup is two-thirds full. Bake for 12 to 15 minutes, until lightly golden and firm to the touch (a toothpick inserted into the center should come out clean).
5. Cool in the pan for 5 minutes, then turn out onto a wire rack to cool completely. Dust with confectioners' sugar before serving.

Nutrition Info:
- Info229 calories; 4 g protein; 15 g total fat; 6 g saturated fat; 22 g carbohydrates; 2 g fiber; 29 mg sodium

Baked Veggie Chips

Servings:6
Cooking Time: 20 Minutes
Ingredients:
- 2 medium parsnips, peeled
- 2 medium zucchini
- 2 medium carrots, peeled
- Olive oil spray
- 1 teaspoon salt, plus more for garnish

Directions:
1. Using a handheld mandoline or a very sharp knife, slice the vegetables into very thin (1/16-inch) rounds.
2. Preheat the oven to 375°F.
3. Lightly oil 2 large baking sheets with olive oil spray.
4. Arrange the sliced vegetables on paper towels in a single layer, season with 1 teaspoon of salt, and let sit for 15 minutes. Dry the vegetables as thoroughly as possible with a paper towel.
5. Arrange the vegetable slices on the baking sheets in a single layer and coat with additional olive oil spray. Bake in the preheated oven for about 20 minutes.
6. Remove the chips from the oven, sprinkle them with additional salt, and let cool for 5 minutes. Serve immediately or cool to room temperature. The chips can then be stored in a sealed container on the countertop for up to 3 days.

Nutrition Info:
- InfoCalories: 86; Protein: 2g; Total Fat: 1g; Saturated Fat: 0g; Carbohydrates: 20g; Fiber: 6g; Sodium: 417mg;

Carrot Cake With Cream Cheese Frosting

Servings:10
Cooking Time:x

Ingredients:

- Nonstick cooking spray
- ⅓ cup (45 g) superfine white rice flour
- ⅓ cup (50 g) cornstarch
- 2 teaspoons gluten-free baking powder
- 1 teaspoon baking soda
- 1 teaspoon xanthan gum or guar gum
- 1 heaping tablespoon ground cinnamon
- 1 heaping tablespoon pumpkin pie spice
- 2 cups (240 g) almond flour
- 1 cup (220 g) packed light brown sugar
- 2 medium carrots, grated
- ⅓ cup (35 g) walnuts, chopped
- 4 large eggs, separated
- One 8-ounce (225 g) package reduced-fat cream cheese
- 1 tablespoon plus 1 teaspoon fresh lemon juice
- ½ cup (80 g) confectioners' sugar

Directions:

1. Preheat the oven to 325°F (160°C). Grease an 8½ x 4½-inch (22 x 15 cm) loaf pan with cooking spray and line with parchment paper, leaving an overhang on the two long sides to help lift out the cake later.

2. Sift the rice flour, cornstarch, baking powder, baking soda, xanthan gum, cinnamon, and pumpkin pie spice three times into a large bowl (or whisk in the bowl until well combined). Stir in the almond flour, brown sugar, grated carrots, walnuts, and egg yolks.

3. Beat the egg whites in a medium bowl with a handheld electric mixer until stiff peaks form. Gently fold the egg whites into the carrot batter with a large metal spoon.

4. Pour the batter into the pan and bake for 45 to 50 minutes, until firm to the touch (a toothpick inserted into the center should come out clean). Cool in the pan for 10 minutes, then turn out onto a wire rack to cool completely.

5. To make the cream cheese frosting, combine the cream cheese, lemon juice, and confectioners' sugar in a bowl and mix until smooth. Spread the frosting over the cooled cake and serve.

Nutrition Info:

- Info384 calories; 11 g protein; 18 g total fat; 5 g saturated fat; 47 g carbohydrates; 4 g fiber; 348 mg sodium

Smoky Eggplant Dip

Servings:2
Cooking Time: 20 Minutes

Ingredients:

- 1 large eggplant (about 1 pound)
- ¼ cup finely chopped fresh flat-leaf parsley, plus more for garnish
- 2 tablespoons creamy peanut butter
- 2 tablespoons lemon juice
- ¼ teaspoon salt
- 2 to 4 tablespoons Garlic Oil (here)
- 1 tablespoon minced fresh parsley
- 1 tablespoon toasted sunflower seeds

Directions:

1. Preheat the oven to 450°F.

2. Line a large baking sheet with aluminum foil. Prick the eggplant all over with the tines of a fork and place it on the prepared baking sheet. Bake in the preheated oven for about 20 minutes, until the skin begins to brown and blister and the flesh inside is soft. Remove from the oven and let sit until cool enough to handle. Halve the eggplant lengthwise and scoop out the flesh, discarding the skin.

3. In a food processor, combine the eggplant flesh, parsley, peanut butter, lemon juice, and salt, and process until smooth. With the processor running, add 2 tablespoons of the Garlic Oil. Add additional oil, if needed, to achieve the desired consistency. Spoon into a serving dish, garnish with parsley, sunflower seeds, and additional Garlic Oil, and serve immediately.

Nutrition Info:

- InfoCalories: 105; Protein: 4g; Total Fat: 5g; Saturated Fat: 1g; Carbohydrates: 11g; Fiber: 6g; Sodium: 200mg;

Ginger Cookies

Servings:20
Cooking Time: 20 Minutes

Ingredients:

- ½ cup warm water
- 2 tbsp chia seeds
- ½ cup brown sugar
- 2 tbsp coconut oil
- 3 tbsp ginger, ground
- 1 tbsp cinnamon
- 1 cup buckwheat flour
- 1 cup brown rice flour
- Peanut butter or dark chocolate for filling

Directions:

1. Preheat the oven to 350°F and line a baking tray with parchment paper.
2. Put the chia seeds into warm water and let sit for 5 minutes.
3. In a bowl, mix the chia seeds and water, sugar, oil, ginger, and cinnamon.
4. Add the flour slowly then create balls with the dough, 1 tablespoon per ball to start with. You can add more dough to make larger cookies. Place them on the baking tray.
5. Make a hole in each ball of dough before baking for 20 minutes.
6. Add the filling while the cookies are still warm.

Nutrition Info:

- Info85g Calories, 3g Total fat, 1.5g Saturated fat, 13g Carbohydrates, 1.8 g Fiber, 2g Protein, 1.8g Sodium.

Dark Chocolate–macadamia Nut Brownies

Servings:18
Cooking Time:x

Ingredients:

- Nonstick cooking spray
- 10 tablespoons (1¼ sticks/150 g) unsalted butter, cut into cubes
- 10½ ounces (300 g) good-quality dark chocolate, broken into pieces
- 1¼ cups (275 g) packed light brown sugar
- ⅔ cup (85 g) superfine white rice flour
- ¼ cup (35 g) cornstarch
- 1 teaspoon xanthan gum or guar gum
- 3 large eggs
- 2 teaspoons vanilla extract
- ½ cup (95 g) dark chocolate chips
- ½ cup (125 ml) light cream
- ¾ cup (100 g) roughly chopped macadamia nuts (optional)

Directions:

1. Preheat the oven to 325°F (160°C). Grease an 11 x 7-inch (29 × 19 cm) baking pan with cooking spray and line with parchment paper.
2. Combine the butter and chocolate in a medium saucepan over low heat and stir until melted and smooth. Add the brown sugar and stir until dissolved. Transfer to a large bowl and let cool to room temperature.
3. Sift the rice flour, cornstarch, and xanthan gum three times into a separate bowl (or whisk in a bowl until well combined).
4. Stir the eggs into the chocolate mixture, one at a time. Add the sifted flour mixture, vanilla, chocolate chips, cream, and macadamia nuts (if using). Mix well, spoon into the baking pan, and smooth the surface.
5. Bake for 20 minutes, then cover with foil and bake for 20 to 25 minutes more, until just firm to the touch.
6. Remove from the oven and let cool in the pan to room temperature. Transfer to the refrigerator for 2 to 3 hours or overnight until firm.
7. Turn out onto a cutting board, peel off the parchment paper, and cut into squares to serve.

Nutrition Info:

- Info278 calories; 3 g protein; 18 g total fat; 9 g saturated fat; 31 g carbohydrates; 2 g fiber; 23 mg sodium

Caramelized Upside-down Banana Cake

Servings: 8
Cooking Time: 25 Minutes

Ingredients:

- Butter or coconut oil for preparing the pan
- 2 tablespoons unsalted butter
- 2 tablespoons brown sugar
- 2 bananas, 1 sliced and 1 mashed, divided
- 2 eggs, lightly beaten
- ⅓ cup maple syrup
- ¼ cup unsweetened coconut milk
- 1 teaspoon vanilla extract
- ½ teaspoon baking soda
- 1 teaspoon distilled vinegar
- ⅓ cup coconut flour

Directions:

1. Preheat the oven to 350°F.
2. Grease a 9-inch cake pan with butter or coconut oil. Put the butter in the cake pan and place the pan in the oven for a few minutes while it is preheating. Once the butter is melted, remove the pan from the oven and tilt it around so that the butter thoroughly coats the bottom of the pan. Sprinkle the brown sugar over the melted butter and arrange the banana slices in the pan on top of the butter and sugar.
3. In a large bowl, combine the eggs, maple syrup, coconut milk, vanilla, baking soda, vinegar, and mashed banana, and mix well. Add the coconut flour, and stir to mix and eliminate any clumps.
4. Pour the batter on top of the banana slices in the pan and spread into an even layer.
5. Bake in the preheated oven until the top of the cake is lightly browned and the cake is set in the center, for about 25 minutes. Remove from the oven and cool completely in the pan on a wire rack.
6. Slide a butter knife around the edge of the cake to loosen it from the pan, then invert the cake onto a serving platter. Serve at room temperature.

Nutrition Info:

- InfoCalories: 173; Protein: 3g; Total Fat: 7g; Saturated Fat: 5g; Carbohydrates: 26g; Fiber: 3g; Sodium: 130mg;

Easy Trail Mix

Servings: 4
Cooking Time: 0 Minutes

Ingredients:

- 1 cup dried bananas
- ½ cup raw unsalted almonds
- ¼ cup raw unsalted peanuts
- ¼ cup dried cranberries

Directions:

1. In a small bowl, mix all the ingredients.
2. Store in a resealable bag at room temperature for up to 1 month.

Nutrition Info:

- InfoCalories:158; Total Fat: 11g; Saturated Fat: 1g; Carbohydrates: 13g; Fiber: 4g; Sodium: 2mg; Protein: 5g

Deviled Eggs

Servings:6
Cooking Time: 0 Minutes
Ingredients:

- 6 hardboiled eggs, peeled and halved lengthwise
- ½ cup Low-FODMAP Mayonnaise
- 2 tablespoons Dijon mustard
- 3 scallions, green parts only, minced
- ½ teaspoon sea salt
- ½ teaspoon ground paprika
- ⅛ teaspoon freshly ground black pepper

Directions:

1. Into a small bowl, scoop the egg yolks from the whites. Set the whites aside.
2. Add the mayonnaise, mustard, scallions, salt, paprika, and pepper to the yolks and mash them with a fork.
3. Spoon the mixture back into the egg whites.

Nutrition Info:

- InfoCalories:240; Total Fat: 18g; Saturated Fat: 4g; Carbohydrates: 11g; Fiber: 1g; Sodium: 537mg; Protein: 10g

Rice Pudding

Servings:4
Cooking Time: 17 Minutes
Ingredients:

- 2 cups unsweetened almond milk, divided
- 1½ cups cooked white rice
- ⅓ cup sugar
- Pinch sea salt
- 1 egg, beaten
- ½ teaspoon vanilla extract
- Freshly grated nutmeg, for garnishing (optional)

Directions:

1. In a medium saucepan over medium heat, stir together 1½ cups almond milk, the rice, sugar, and salt. Cover and cook for about 15 minutes, or until thick.
2. Add the remaining ½ cup almond milk and the egg. Cook for 2 minutes, stirring constantly.
3. Remove the pan from the heat and stir in the vanilla.
4. Serve warm garnished with freshly grated nutmeg (if using).

Nutrition Info:

- InfoCalories:49; Total Fat: 2g; Saturated Fat: 0g; Carbohydrates: 7g; Fiber: <1g; Sodium: 91mg; Protein: <1g

Lemon Tart

Servings:8
Cooking Time:x
Ingredients:

- Nonstick cooking spray
- 1 cup (130 g) superfine white rice flour
- ½ cup (75 g) cornstarch, plus more for kneading
- ½ cup (45 g) soy flour
- 1 teaspoon xanthan gum or guar gum
- ¼ cup (55 g) superfine sugar
- 10 tablespoons (1¼ sticks/150 g) cold unsalted butter, diced

- About ½ cup (100 to 125 ml) ice water
- ¾ cup (165 g) superfine sugar
- One 8-ounce (225 g) package mascarpone (1 cup)
- 1 heaping tablespoon finely grated lemon zest
- ⅔ cup (165 ml) fresh lemon juice
- 4 large eggs
- Confectioners' sugar, for dusting

Directions:

1. Preheat the oven to 350°F (180°C). Grease a 9-inch (23 cm) fluted tart pan with cooking spray.
2. To make the crust, sift the rice flour, cornstarch, soy flour, and xanthan gum into a bowl. Transfer to a food processor, add the superfine sugar and butter, and process until the mixture resembles fine bread crumbs. While the motor is running, add the ice water (a tablespoon at a time) to form a soft dough.
3. Lightly sprinkle your work surface with cornstarch. Turn out the dough onto the work surface and knead until smooth. Wrap in plastic wrap and refrigerate for 30 minutes.
4. Place the dough between two sheets of parchment paper and roll out to a thickness of about ⅛ inch (2 to 3 mm). Ease the crust into the pan and trim the edges to neaten.
5. Line the crust with parchment paper, fill with pie weights or rice, and bake for 10 minutes, or until lightly golden. Remove the weights and parchment. Reduce the oven temperature to 325°F (160°C).
6. To make the filling, combine the superfine sugar, mascarpone, lemon zest, and lemon juice in a medium bowl and beat with a handheld electric mixer. Add the eggs one at a time, beating well between additions. Pour the filling into the warm crust and bake for 30 to 35 minutes, until set.
7. Cool completely in the pan. Dust with confectioners' sugar before serving.

Nutrition Info:

- Info408 calories; 8 g protein; 24 g total fat; 8 g saturated fat; 42 g carbohydrates; 1 g fiber; 50 mg sodium

Maple-spiced Walnuts

Servings:2
Cooking Time: 8 Minutes
Ingredients:

- 2 tablespoons maple syrup
- 2 teaspoons olive oil
- 1 tablespoon water
- 2 cups walnut halves
- 1 tablespoon sugar
- 1 teaspoon coarse salt
- 1 teaspoon ground cumin
- ½ teaspoon ground coriander
- ⅛ teaspoon cayenne pepper

Directions:

1. Combine the maple syrup, oil, and water in a large skillet. Heat, stirring, over medium heat for about 5 minutes. Stir in the walnuts.
2. Add the sugar, salt, cumin, coriander, and cayenne pepper. Cook, tossing to coat the nuts well, for about 3 minutes more, until the nuts are lightly browned.
3. Transfer to a sheet of parchment paper, spread the nuts out into a single layer, separate them, and cool completely. Serve at room temperature.

Nutrition Info:

- InfoCalories: 223; Protein: 8g; Total Fat: 20g; Saturated Fat: 1g; Carbohydrates: 8g; Fiber: 2g; Sodium: 242mg;

Chinese Chicken In Lettuce Cups

Servings:4
Cooking Time: 5 Minutes
Ingredients:
- 2 tablespoons gluten-free soy sauce
- 2 tablespoons rice vinegar
- ½ teaspoon salt
- ½ teaspoon sugar
- 2 tablespoons vegetable oil
- 2 teaspoons Garlic Oil (here)
- 2 teaspoons minced fresh ginger
- 1 pound boneless, skinless chicken breasts, minced
- ½ cup water chestnuts, minced
- 8 to 10 inner leaves iceberg lettuce, edges trimmed and chilled
- Handful of fresh cilantro leaves, coarsely chopped
- ¼ cup unsalted roasted peanuts, coarsely chopped (optional)

Directions:
1. In a small bowl, stir together the soy sauce, rice vinegar, salt, and sugar.
2. Heat the vegetable oil and Garlic Oil in a skillet or wok set over high heat. Add the ginger and cook, stirring, for 10 seconds. Add the chicken and cook, stirring, for about 1 minute, until the chicken is opaque all over. Add the water chestnuts and reduce to medium-low. Stir in the soy sauce mixture and cook for about 2 minutes more, until the chicken is cooked through.
3. Arrange the lettuce cups on a platter or serving plates and spoon some of the chicken mixture into each, dividing equally. Garnish each serving with cilantro and peanuts, if using, and serve immediately.

Nutrition Info:
- InfoCalories: 378; Protein: 36g; Total Fat: 19g; Saturated Fat: 4g; Carbohydrates: 14g; Fiber: 1g; Sodium: 778mg;

Quinoa Muffins

Servings:24
Cooking Time: 20 Minutes
Ingredients:
- 1 ½ cups quinoa flour
- 1 cup quinoa flakes
- ⅓ cup walnuts, chopped
- 1 tbsp cinnamon
- 4 tsp baking powder
- 2 tsp baking soda
- Pinch of salt
- 4 eggs
- 4 bananas, mashed
- ½ cup almond milk
- ¼ cup maple syrup

Directions:
1. Preheat the oven to 375°F.
2. Mix the dry ingredients in one bowl. In a separate bowl, combine the wet ingredients. Combine the ingredients until mixed fully.
3. Spoon into greased muffin pans and bake for 20 minutes. Check if the center is dry by poking the center of a muffin with a skewer. If it comes out clean, they are ready.

Nutrition Info:
- Info175g Calories, 10.5g Total fat, 4g Saturated fat, 6g Carbohydrates, 1.5 g Fiber, 14g Protein, 4g Sodium.

APPENDIX : Recipes Index

Chocolate Fudge Sauce 76
Chocolate Peanut Butter Cups 75
Chocolate Soufflés 72
Chopped Italian Salad 55
Citrusy Swordfish Skewers 25
Classic Coleslaw 59
Clever Curry Mayonnaise 66
Coconut Shrimp 20
Coconut-curry Tofu With Vegetables 47
Coq Au Vin 38
Creamy Halibut 16
Crispy Rice Balls With Parmesan And Corn 10
Crustless Spinach Quiche 44
Cumin Turkey With Fennel 33
Curried Potato And Parsnip Soup 60

D

Dark Chocolate–macadamia Nut Brownies 79
Deviled Eggs 81
Dill Dipping Sauce 67

E

Easy Breakfast Sausage 11
Easy Rice Pilaf 62
Easy Trail Mix 80
Egg-free Caesar Dressing 67
Eggplant Bacon 13

F

Fennel Pomegranate Salad 53
Feta Crab Cakes 25
Filet Mignon Salad 53
Fish And Chips 26
Fish And Potato Pie 27
Fried Eggs With Potato Hash 9

G

Garden Pesto 64
Ginger Cookies 79
Ginger-berry Rice Milk Smoothie 5
Glazed Salmon 15
Glorious Strawberry Salad 56
Goat Cheese And Potato Tacos With Red Chili Cream Sauce 46
Green Smoothie 6
Grilled Cod With Fresh Basil 16
Grilled Halibut With Lemony Pesto 24

Grilled Swordfish With Pineapple Salsa 23

H

Hawaiian Toasted Sandwich 12
Hazelnut Or Almond Crescents 75

I

Italian Vegetable Sauce 69

K

Kale Sesame Salad With Tamari-ginger Dressing 57

L

Lemon Bar 74
Lemon Tart 82
Lemon-pepper Shrimp 34
Lentil Chili 58
Light Tuna Casserole 21
Lime Pork Stir-fry With Rice Noodles 27
Low-fodmap Hummus 73
Low-fodmap Mayonnaise 71
Low-fodmap Vegetable Broth 63
Luscious Hot Fudge Sauce 68

M

Mac 'n' Cheeze 47
Maple Mustard Dipping Sauce 71
Maple-glazed Salmon 24
Maple-spiced Walnuts 82
Mashed Potatoes 56
Mediterranean Crustless Quiche 13
Mediterranean Flaky Fish With Vegetables 18
Mediterranean Noodles 49
Mixed Berry & Yogurt Granola Bar 5
Mussels In Chili, Bacon, And Tomato Broth 52

O

Orange Chicken And Broccoli Stir-fry 33
Orange-ginger Salmon 35
Orange-maple Glazed Carrots 54
Overnight Carrot Cake Oats And Walnuts 12
Oysters, Three Ways 8

P

Pan-seared Scallops With Sautéed Kale 32

Pasta With Pesto Sauce 42

Pesto Sauce 70

Pesto Toasted Sandwich 9

Pineapple Fried Rice 45

Pineapple Salsa 73

Pineapple, Yogurt On Rice Cakes 72

Pork And Vegetable Fricassee With Buttered Quinoa 36

Pork Loin Rub 65

Potato Pancakes 5

Potato Soup 60

Prosciutto-wrapped Cantaloupe 73

Pumpkin Cornbread 61

Pumpkin Pie Pancakes 14

Q

Quiche In Ham Cups 8

Quinoa Breakfast Bowl With Basil "hollandaise" Sauce 10

Quinoa Muffins 83

Quinoa With Swiss Chard 57

Quinoa-stuffed Eggplant Roulades With Feta And Mint 41

R

Raspberry Sauce 68

Red Snapper With Creole Sauce 31

Rice Pudding 81

Rita's Linguine With Clam Sauce 23

Roasted Garlic Shrimp And Red Peppers 31

Roasted Potato Wedges 55

S

Salmon Noodle Casserole 15

Savory Baked Tofu 43

Seafood Risotto 22

Shrimp And Cheese Casserole 16

Shrimp Bisque 62

Shrimp Puttanesca With Linguine 19

Shrimp With Cherry Tomatoes 19

Smoky Corn Chowder With Red Peppers 44

Smoky Eggplant Dip 78

Sole Meunière 18

Soy-infused Roast Chicken 32

Spanish Meatloaf With Garlic Mashed Potatoes 37

Spanish Rice 43

Spinach And Bell Pepper Salad With Fried Tofu Puffs 52

Printed in Great Britain
by Amazon

26177823R00057